The Legacy of
Irish Missionaries
Lives On

ISBN: 978 1 897685 55 6

Published in Ireland 2016 by Onstream Publications, Currabaha, Cloghroe, County Cork, Ireland.
www.onstream.ie

Book design and production: Nick Sanquest

Printed by City Print Ltd., Cork, Ireland

The Legacy of
Irish Missionaries
Lives On

Matt Moran

MATT MORAN

ON STREAM

Acknowledgements

This book was inspired by my interaction with hundreds of missionaries over the years, but the principal catalyst was the visionary speakers at the Mission Today & Tomorrow Conference which I helped to organise in All Hallows College, Dublin in 2013.

Many organisations and individuals have helped in creating this publication. I thank the IMU (now AMRI) and Trócaire for their generous financial support and for their encouragement and trust.

Congregations, individual missionaries, and others willingly gave of their time to provide material and photographs when asked. Not all congregations get the same billing, but this should not be seen as a slight on the work of those not mentioned. This book is not a history of congregations.

I thank those who contributed articles or short reflections that add greatly to the text. In particular, I thank those from outside of the missionary movement for their insightful contributions that give an external perspective.

Dr. Kevin O'Sullivan, NUI Galway, was generous in sharing his material, as was Peter O'Mahony, Spiritan Communications, Sr. Catherine Hally MSHR, Archivist, Holy Rosary Sisters, Áine McHugh, Archivist, Loreto Irish Province and Sr. Joan Hally MSHR who facilitated guided access to IMU records of the early 1970s.

Publishers of earlier books – Joe Humphreys, Ronan Murphy, Irene Lynch, Fr. Richard Quinn CSSp, Dr. Edmund Hogan SMA, Fr. Hugh McMahon SSC, and Aidan and Brendan Clerkin – were supportive in allowing me to use extracts from their publications.

I am honoured that Mary Robinson wrote the thoughtful Foreword that is positioned nicely in her address, as President of Ireland, to the IMU in 1993, and eloquently updated to the present.

Sr. Louis Mary O'Connor SJC and Maureen O'Dwyer read the draft and gave pertinent comments which I appreciated. My wife, Geraldine, was a constant source of encouragement and advice throughout the project.

My choice of Roz Crowley of Onstream Publications as my publisher was prudent. She and her team were both efficient and friendly to work with. Drawing on her professionalism and experience, she provided much sound advice.

I thank everyone who contributed in any way to this publication. It has been a great exercise in collaboration.

Matt Moran

Dedication

I dedicate this book to the many thousands of Irish missionaries and lay volunteers, past and present, who brought faith, hope and love to people in the Global South, and to their successors who are continuing their legacy with the same core values of justice, respect, integrity, compassion and commitment.

Impact of the Irish abroad

Irish
MISSIONARIES

ÉIRE   CLÚDACH CHÉAD LAE   ≋POST

An Post issued two postage stamps on 21 June 1991 to recognise the impact of Irish missionaries overseas. One stamp depicted a missionary providing medical treatment, and the other depicted missionaries working at a water pump, representing two of the essential services that missionaries provide in deprived communities in the Global South

Contents

Foreword

When, as President of Ireland, I addressed a meeting of the Irish Missionary Union in St. Patrick's College, Maynooth on 16 October 1993, I said, "The role of the missionary has changed quite substantially since Father Joseph Shanahan first arrived in Nigeria in 1903, but the basic values which motivate you and inspire your work have not." Over the 23 years since then, the structure of the Irish missionary movement has changed very substantially due to the decline in vocations to religious life in Ireland and Europe, but again, the basic values that motivate and inspire missionaries have not changed, irrespective of their country of birth.

This book reflects on the great humanitarian and development work of missionaries and gives lots of examples and a few case histories. It differs from other books about missionaries by illustrating how the missionary era that we have been familiar with, from primary school onwards, has changed. It tells how local and indigenous missionaries are now carrying forward the legacy of the Irish missionaries with the same passion and commitment in poor and deprived communities, and during natural disasters or emergencies where they are first responders. Most of these local missionaries are members of congregations with bases in Ireland, but many are also diocesan congregations founded by the Irish and are a key part of the Irish legacy.

Told by a lay insider the story is easy to read. Matt Moran has an in-depth knowledge of the missionary movement. Having headed up fundraising and development for the Missionaries of the Sacred Heart for ten years, he then served on the board of Misean Cara for five years with four of these as chairman. Using that experience and knowledge of missionaries, he has thoughtfully brought together in this book the views of academics, leaders of church and state, development specialists, media personnel, historians, and diplomats as well as missionaries and the people they support in the developing world. Their shared experiences provide a wealth of knowledge and insight into the truly remarkable contribution and impact that our missionaries have made, and are continuing to make, alongside their successors and partners in the developing world.

The book gives new insights into the role played by missionaries in the setting up of APSO in the early 1970s, and which led on quickly to the establishment of Ireland's overseas aid programme in 1974. It is acknowledged by the state that that programme was greatly influenced by the work of missionaries in earlier decades. They were the early pioneers who provided services in education and health, in rural development, the provision of drinking water and sanitation services, and tackling the root causes of poverty and injustice. They were the ambassadors who brought home the stories about conditions in the developing world. Those stories helped the Irish people to empathise with the great need to provide help through missionaries themselves, and through NGOs and the aid programme. Congregations built up hundreds of thousands of supporters around Ireland, and this mass movement greatly influenced popular support for the Irish aid programme.

The author has taken great care in presenting a deep understanding of the intrinsic values that faith brings to development and humanitarian aid. I am very pleased to see the increasingly important role being played by faith-based organisations at the United Nations. Religious leaders are now more at the heart of global decision-making where, through their extensive networks in the developing world, they advocate for living conditions there, abuses in civil rights and social justice, and climate change.

Missionaries have long since been advocates for protection of nature and the environment as God's creation. In *Laudato Si'*, Pope Francis shows his profound understanding of the connection between nature, justice for people living in poverty, human dignity and the need to act in solidarity in the face of climate change. Above all else, he establishes climate change and safeguarding the earth for humanity as the moral issue of our time. Climate justice is a major global issue that requires the greatest solidarity by all sectors. Missionaries, religious leaders, and the newly established *Global Catholic Climate Movement,* made up of hundreds of organisations globally, can make a highly valuable contribution to this global effort and to the Sustainable Development Goals.

As the shift in Christianity from the north to the south impacts the number and visibility of missionaries in Ireland, this traditional connection between Ireland and developing countries is declining. Using his experience in town twinning and supporting it with interesting case histories, Matt Moran demonstrates how parish twinning is an innovative model of partnership in international relations and a bridge that can connect communities in Ireland and the Global South.

Many missionaries are passionate leaders in tackling issues of gender equality and improving the welfare of women in developing countries. Both directly and through their networks, they focus on education for the girl child, female genital mutilation, pregnancy and child-birth services, early marriage of girls, the vulnerability of women and girls, especially in human trafficking, and psycho-social supports during crises such as Ebola and HIV.

In a male dominated institutional church, missionary sisters have played an important role in the provision of pastoral services, and involvement of the laity in community and parish activities. In Africa, many sisters are now engaging in the study of theology up to doctoral level. This book shows how priests and sisters are showing leadership in inter-faith dialogue which is becoming increasingly important in our world with so many conflicts.

Missionaries are an important part of our diaspora. Their committed work, as illustrated dispassionately in the book and supported with diverse testimonial evidence, has helped to establish a recognition of Irish values internationally. The missionary movement is firmly enshrined as a key part of our national heritage. This book commends the past, and points to the future where the work of the Irish will be continued in a new era by local and indigenous missionaries and by Irish lay missionary volunteers.

It will be a valuable resource for historians and documentary makers, for students undertaking research, for those interested in international development and volunteering, and for media personnel, as well as the general reader. I am pleased to recommend this book.

Mary Robinson
President, Mary Robinson Foundation for Climate Justice

Mary Robinson was President of Ireland from 1990-1997, and UN High Commissioner for Human Rights from 1997-2002. She was founder and President of Realising Rights: The Ethical Globalisation Initiative from 2002 – 2010. In 2016 she was appointed UN Special Envoy on El Niño and Climate.

Mary Robinson and her husband, Nick, meeting Sr. Martha McDermott MSHR in São Paulo, Brazil in 1995

Holy Rosary Sisters

Introduction

One of the great achievements of the Irish nation on the world stage has been the remarkable contribution of Irish missionaries to the poor and marginalised in the Global South. Many books have been written and films made about this missionary movement comprised of missionaries, their families, supporters, lay missionary volunteers, apostolic workers, and the wider Irish public through their material and prayerful support. These books and films are a historical and social record of the lives and works of many individual missionaries and congregations over numerous decades in over 90 countries.

These earlier books are a foundation for this publication which focuses on the legacy of the Irish missionaries and how it is being continued by a new generation in the Global South. It captures a miscellany of views and perspectives on an extraordinary movement. It reflects on the past and the present in order to look to the future.

Evangelisation is the essence of the Catholic Church, and is synonymous with missionary efforts. Vatican II (1962 – 1965) introduced a new understanding of mission, proclaiming that the church by its very nature is missionary and all the baptised are called to participate in its mission. Catholics are called to read the signs of the times, that is, together discern God's movement in the world. The goal now is to engage with people of other faiths, and to serve and to empower people with the Christian message, thereby enabling them to flourish and to transform themselves and their communities within the context of the equality of races and nations.

Irish missionaries were quick to respond positively to this new understanding of mission. Some of them were doing mission that way already. The Irish understood oppression and colonisation, and the plight of the poor based on our own history. They understood the significance of the word of God in the world.

The *Mission Conference* held in Dalgan, Co. Meath in 1968 had the theme *The Church's Mission*. This was followed by the setting up of the Irish Missionary Union (IMU) in 1970 as a collaborative network of 85 missionary sending congregations and two lay missionary sending organisations. In 1979, the *National Mission Congress* and exhibition was held at Knock Shrine with the theme *A New Missionary Era*, and attracted several thousand participants over eight days. These events helped to advance a broader understanding of mission.

Today, the Vatican II understanding of mission is at the heart of Pope Francis' Pontificate which is an inspiration for missionaries. Pope Francis reminds us that we are all called to be 'missionary disciples of Jesus'.

In earlier decades, missionaries interpreted their role in accordance with their understanding of their times. The charism of many congregations refers to meeting needs in accordance with 'the signs of the times'. For example, the mission statement of the Irish Spiritans states that their "preaching has different styles differentiated by the times and the places we are living in."

Like with many other aspects of Irish life today, some commentators have a tendency to describe earlier mission purely within the terms of today's interpretation and understanding. Such reading back ignores that the world of mission has moved on. Missionaries are on a learning curve too, especially since Vatican II.

This learning does not reside only with Catholic missionaries. The Church Mission Society of the Anglican Church says, "Over time, things change," and it has "seen significant developments in the understanding of mission and of the world beyond our shores."

Generally, Catholic missionaries were early practitioners of ecumenism, and were respectful of local cultures. Many of them learned the local languages as recognition of the culture of their host communities. The Spiritan's mission statement of 1987 is clear on culture and ecumenism. It states: "So that the Christian witness may become integrated in the culture, reach people from within, and become a force for liberation in their contemporary history, we strive in every way we can for a fruitful coming together of local culture and religious traditions within the gospel of Christ."

That ethos is reflected in the statement of strategic intent of Misean Cara in the words: "Our purpose is to be in solidarity with the poor in ways that transforms lives while respecting the integrity of local cultures."

Pope Benedict XVI in an encyclical letter *Deus Caritas Est* (No. 25.a) in December 2005 dealing with the service of charity in the church said: "The Church's deepest nature is expressed in her three-fold responsibility of proclaiming the word of God, celebrating the sacraments, and exercising the ministry of charity. These duties presuppose each other and are inseparable. For the Church, charity is not a kind of welfare activity which could equally well be left to others, but is a part of her nature, an indispensable expression of her very being."

Archbishop Peter Fanyana Butelezi OMI from Blomfontein in South Africa speaking at the *National Mission Congress* in 1979 said, "It is important that missionaries be involved in development, otherwise, many people will see them as a paternalistic group … through involvement in development, the foreign missionaries can build up a whole nation … involvement in development is a proclamation that we have confidence in the people we work for and that we have come to serve." Referring to the empowerment of local people, he said: "Through the help of foreign missionaries the local people will in time have their own leaders who will then plan and supervise the progress of the work."

The Anglican Church holds, "There is no division between the words of the gospel and the works of the gospel, between proclamation and social action." This book focuses on the integral human development dimension of mission as a sign of the sharing of all the faithful in the mission of the Church.

Christianity as a percentage of the population in the global north is declining. Since the twentieth century we have experienced the great shift of Christianity to the Global South. A consequence of this in the Catholic Church has been a decline in vocations to religious life in the north and an increase in the south. Following from that, those that were missionary receiving countries are now becoming missionary sending countries themselves as the geography of mission shifts. Mission knows of no fixed abode or geographical limitations.

The Pontifical Yearbook 2016 and the Annuarium Statisticum Ecclesiae 2014 shows that the number of priests globally increased by 9,381 from 406,411 to 415,792 between 2005 and 2014. In Africa and Asia there was an increase of 33% and 27% respectively, whereas in Europe the number declined by 8% during that period. Africa and Asia also showed an increase of 7.5% in women religious, and non-ordained male religious numbers grew in Africa by 10% and in Asia by 30% with both categories decreasing in Europe. The largest increase in the number of Catholics was also in Africa and Asia. On the social side, the Catholic Church ran 71,188 kindergartens, 95,246 primary and 43,783 secondary schools, 1,358 universities and institutes of higher education, and 115,353 healthcare and related centres throughout the world.

There is also a significant paradigm shift around faith and development involving global bodies such as the United Nations, World Health Organisation, and the World Bank, as well as governments in the north like Great Britain, Germany, Sweden, the Netherlands, and the USA. The work and role of faith-inspired organisations in the areas of development, humanitarian aid, and climate justice is now being embraced strongly by these, as it has been in Ireland for many decades through our missionaries who were pioneering ambassadors for the country.

The Catholic Church, like many other faiths, has promoted care of the earth for decades. In this, many missionaries have been to the forefront. Pope Francis' first encyclical, *Laudato Si'*, issued in 2015 was focused on the idea of 'integral ecology', connecting care of the natural world with justice for the poorest and most vulnerable people, and moved this care from the periphery of the church into the centre. This shift, and the UN Paris decisions on climate change in December

2015, has given a new impetus to missionaries. It brings vast opportunities for new initiatives and collaboration at many levels that help to restore the centrality of the common good and allows Catholic social teaching to offer a path towards authentic human flourishing in the context of the modern global economy.

These shifts in Christianity, in development, and in care of the earth bring new opportunities that animate missionaries and lift their spirits as they discover how they can share and contribute to the betterment of all in the service of God.

Against that background, this book reflects on the work that Irish missionaries and their partners have been doing, and continue to do, in the Global South. As Irish-born missionaries now active in developing countries number just over 1,100, the views of some local missionaries presented here indicate how they see mission today and into the future.

The book points to the role and influence of missionaries in the evolution of Ireland's overseas aid initiatives in the 1970s, and describes the expanding role of faith in international development, and how governments and secular agencies are embracing that role. Also described is the very significant work on advocacy for human rights and social justice that many congregations undertake collaboratively at the United Nations.

A key message of the book is to demonstrate how the legacy of the Irish is being carried forward by the new generations of local and indigenous missionaries, by lay missionary volunteers from Ireland, and by local or diocesan congregations founded by Irish missionaries in Africa and in India. Another important message is to explain the benefits of parish twinning as an important link between communities in Ireland and in developing countries.

The book illustrates how missionary development work is an integral part of Ireland's overseas aid programme to which it adds unique value, and how some other European countries are now searching for that unique value to support their development programmes. In conclusion, the book presents the case why this work should continue to be an integral part of the Irish aid programme into the future.

The contributors to this book from different backgrounds and countries bring diversity in message, language and tone. Their collective knowledge and experience of the Irish missionary movement enriches the content. I hope you enjoy reading it as much as I enjoyed researching and bringing it all together within these covers.

Matt Moran, October 2016

Chapter One

The Legacy of Irish Missionaries in the Global South

"Your people have spread love for the Catholic church everywhere they went in every century of your history. This has been done by the earliest monks and the missionaries of Europe's dark ages, by the refugees from persecution, by the exiles, and by the missionaries – men and women – of the last century and this one." So spoke Pope John Paul II in the Phoenix Park in Dublin on 29 September 1979.

The legacy of the Irish missionaries is immense – both in terms of spreading the gospel message of Jesus Christ and undertaking development and humanitarian activities in over 90 countries worldwide. Many books have been written on aspects of this long history. This chapter gives a brief overview of the legacy. Here, five guest authors give their views on the past and the present. The next three chapters will continue the story.

I

The Irish Missionary Movement has been a Subject for Books and Films
Ruan Magan

The Irish missionary movement is arguably the most significant contribution that Ireland made to the world during its first 50 years of independence. Over five decades, between 1920 and 1970, more than 30,000 men and women joined missionary orders, both Irish and continental, and travelled deep into the developing world bringing their faith, charity and skills to the poorest of the world. Between 1930 and 1960, Ireland became, on a per capita basis, the largest source of Catholic missionaries in the world.

Several books have been published around the subject. Most however, written by missionaries over the years were not directed towards a popular audience. By far the most accessible is Joe Humphreys' *God's Entrepreneurs*, which looks at some of the most interesting characters of the last thirty years of the movement. Fr. Edmund Hogan's *The Irish Missionary Movement* is the only book to attempt to take on an overview of the history.

Of greater interest are the many documentary films that have been made since

A typical African scene – a Malawian woman collecting water   *Sally McEllistrim, World Missions Ireland*

the 1920s. Of particular note is Andrew Buchanan's incredible film, *The Visitation* produced in the early 1930s for the Medical Missionaries of Mary. The Holy Rosary Sisters also commissioned films dating from the late 1920s onwards which show the young sisters travelling to Africa and working on the missions. These films and others can be found in the Irish Film Archive.

Radharc made many fascinating films that focused on missionaries beginning in 1965 with a trip to Kenya. Of particular note are: *Turkana (Flying Medical Missionary Nuns)*, *Night Flight to Uli (Biafran Civil War)*, *These Men Are Dangerous (Liberation Theology in Brazil)*, *Father of the Red Bull (an Irish priest going native)* and *Pain is the Price (Shay Cullen as a young man)*. In all, Radharc made 420 films of which about 150 were filmed with the missionaries abroad.

During the last six years I've had the honour of making several documentaries around the subject: *On God's Mission* (two-part documentary overview on the history of the movement), *The Radharc Squad* (two-part documentary on the history of Radharc), *The Nazarene* (a documentary about Fr. Charlie Burrows in Indonesia), and *Lifers* (documentary about three elderly missionaries at work today). Copies are available through Tyrone Productions.

Ruan Magan is an award-winning writer and filmmaker based in Dublin. He has made several documentaries about the Irish missionary movement and individual missionaries.

II
They Represent the Very Best in Us
Patsy McGarry

In November 2014, I reported on President Michael D Higgins's visit to Ethiopia, Malawi, and South Africa. For this occasionally jaundiced Irishman it was a heartening experience. So much of the best in our people is daily experience there. Meeting Irish missionaries in those countries felt like rejuvenation.

There was Kiltegan priest, Fr. Gus Frawley, from Clare. He has been in Malawi 44 years since he was expelled from Biafra in 1970. And Sister of Charity Imelda O'Brien, who has been in Malawi two years, after 33 years in Zambia and nine years in Nigeria. They were among six Irish missionaries who have spent their adult lives serving the poorest of the poor in Africa and who were honoured at a dinner in Malawi attended by President Higgins and his wife, Sabina, hosted by Ambassador Áine Hearns.

Days beforehand in Ethiopia, the President and Mrs Higgins visited an eye clinic in Mekele run by the Daughters of Charity and sponsored by Trócaire. Sr. Margaret Coyne, sister of Mrs Higgins, had worked there for 23 years.

The following week at Soweto's Regina Mundi Catholic Church in South Africa we heard eight Irish nuns speak passionately about the need for more education there. Among them was Sr. Frances Sheehy from Limerick, in South Africa for 43 years.

What was so striking about these missionaries in all three countries was their deep love for the local people and an abiding and passionate commitment to their welfare. This, despite decades of service behind them already in the great majority of cases. They had not wearied.

Speaking in Ethiopia President Higgins said of them all: "To me they represent an 'Irishness' to which all of us should aspire, motivated by a deep empathy put into action and a strong ethical character." They represent the very best in us.

Patsy McGarry is Religious Affairs Correspondent with the Irish Times

III
How Missionaries Magnify the Impact of their Work
Lucy Franks

One of my favourite pieces of music is Shaun Davey's 'The Brendan Voyage', a telling of a transatlantic voyage that was homage to the legendary sailing of the missionary St. Brendan from Ireland to America. Though St. Brendan's pioneering voyage is perhaps a romanticism, the missionary heritage of Ireland in fact traces back as far as the 6th century, when Irish monks such as Columba were sent abroad to found monasteries and centres of education and spirituality throughout Europe and beyond. Fast forward through centuries of invasions and religious turmoil to the 19th century when a major resurgence in missionary activity from Ireland took place. A significant number of men and women of all Christian denominations joined missionary congregations and movements to work overseas. And in doing so, they opened another window on the wider world for Ireland.

Each continent retains the imprint and legacy of these Irish men and women whose work formed one of the cornerstones of what is now the official Irish overseas aid and development programme. Minister Joe Costello, addressing delegates at the *Mission Today and Tomorrow Conference* stated, "The long tradition and commitment of Irish missionaries has led the way for much of the Irish Government's approach to development. Ireland is renowned for its professional overseas development programme. It is Irish missionary work that has given this programme its solid foundation."

Back then missionaries operated within the context of mass colonisation and the trend was for improvement in mainstream education and health standards, as well as religious education. Indeed in many developing countries today, state service provision of education and health has its foundation in missionary-run services. The WHO estimates that 30-70% of the sprawling healthcare infrastructure across the African continent is owned or run by FBOs, with percentages varying within this range in different countries.

Following decolonisation during the latter half of the twentieth century, 'development' emerged as a response to concerns around economic conditions in the former colony countries. Over time the definition has broadened to incorporate many social disciplines. Within the development context today, there are multiple flavours and approaches. One such approach is 'faith based' which generally implies that one's faith (and its associated values) is a motivating factor guiding development interventions.

Missionaries today express core faith values of justice, respect, integrity, compassion and commitment through their work and presence with poor, marginalised and vulnerable communities in the developing world. Their role as development actors has evolved considerably over the years. Whilst retaining their core expertise in the fields of education and health, they also undertake a wide range of complementary activities in the areas of human rights, peace-building, income generation and livelihoods, advocacy and ecological integrity. One could liken them to 'force multipliers', enabling the communities with whom they work and live to

Fr. Pat Galvin MSC has supported the drilling of wells in South Africa   *Fr. James Mitchell MSC*

9

actively assert their human rights, overcome poverty and create a sustainable future.

There is a number of facets to missionary development work which magnify the impact and effectiveness of their interventions for the communities they serve. These are:

The role of trust: Missionaries are present and involved with communities for a sustained time period, and frequently, where other actors may find it difficult to work, such as remote areas, climate-challenged regions, areas of insecurity, war and severe impoverishment, or with groups that are 'hard to reach' in terms of challenging to engage with, or those facing additional barriers associated with marginalisation and stigma. This accompaniment approach engenders trust within communities who become confident that they will not be abandoned. Trust is a pre-requisite for successful development interventions.

Understanding community needs and competence in delivery: Their commitment to presence in communities for a long time fosters an incremental development approach and culture of learning. So, just as missionaries are trusted by the communities in which they work, they also retain significant credibility with state and church actors and other strategic partners, who, recognising their competence and experience, will partner with them in provision of essential services. Missionaries are frequently invited to conduct needs assessments in impoverished communities and to work together with those communities to determine and deliver relevant, effective and high quality interventions over time as the needs of these communities evolve.

An holistic approach to development: Within the missionary context, holistic development, which focuses on all key development needs of the person, is a factor in deepening the quality of change realised. There is a strong sense of care and respect for the integrity of the person. Many missionary development projects consist of complementary interventions so that a more comprehensive set of services can meet differing needs of beneficiaries, and result in high quality impactful change.

Catalytic role in humanitarian or security emergencies: In humanitarian or security emergencies missionaries are frequently first responders because they are already there, and after the media spotlight wanes, play a catalytic role in the longer-term recovery. Through their approach and methods of delivery, longer-term empowerment and resilience are encouraged in affected communities.

As Olivia Wilkinson points out in *Faith and Resilience after Disaster,* published by Misean Cara in 2015: "It is the long-term outlook that set the missionary organisations apart from other actors and ensured their impact on community resilience. These organisations were present before the emergency, assisted during the emergency, and could also be relied on to stay helping the community into the future, after the emergency ... Again, this was a sign of compassion and care that marked a crucial difference between FBOs and non-FBOs in participants' eyes."

Advocacy and networking: Missionaries, through their networks, play a significant role within the faith-based community in advocating for human rights and social justice at community, national and international level, influencing the shape of policies and legislation. They amplify the voices of the people with whom they live and work. Many missionary organisations have a presence at UN level, and played an influential role during the evolution of the Sustainable Development Goals.

Moving over but remaining connected through their local members: The dream of every missionary is in time to move on to places of greater need and move over so that local people take on ownership and responsibility for institutions and works. The present reality witnesses to this through successful succession in leadership to local members. So many local members are now 'running the show', assisted by local workers, and the Irish missionary is often in the background as a resource person and a real supportive contact for the local members.

Motivation and promotion of lay participation: An often overlooked aspect of missionary development is the motivation it inspires in others, whether it is as volunteers at home in Ireland who promote missionary work and fundraise for missionaries who grew up in their communities or through parish and diocesan twinning arrangements, or volunteers abroad working with them as associates or project workers. It is this group of lay people working abroad who together with local missionaries in the Global South are becoming the future of mission.

We frequently hear about the legacy of Irish missionaries, as if their work is now reaching a finite conclusion. It is true that in parallel with the decline in religious vocations in Ireland, the predominance of Irish-born religious missionaries is waning. It has been in the nature of Irish missionaries to build local capacity, to in effect work themselves out of the frame, to ensure that others take up and help realise their vision for a world in which all have the opportunity to live life to the full.

Irish missionaries are still in the Global South – both lay and religious – from all Christian traditions, filling gaps where needs exist, and working alongside thousands of local missionaries who are refining and building on the legacies of those who went before. So the story has not concluded, but a different and exciting chapter is beginning as new generations come of age.

Lucy Franks is Chairperson of the Board of Misean Cara.

IV
Trócaire and Irish Missionaries 1973 – 2016
Éamonn Meehan

'Trócaire is one of the things that make me proud to be Irish. It is a Church organisation that both feeds the poor and asks the difficult question: "Why are they poor?" – Fr. Niall O'Brien, Columban missionary.

Trócaire was born in the turbulent 1970s, at a time when massive inflation and double-figure interest rates damaged the economies of many fragile, post-colonial, resource-rich countries and plunged them into poverty at an unprecedented level. Irish missionaries were already hard at work in the heart of these countries in the 'Third World' as the Global South was then called, ministering to the sick, the poor, and the disenfranchised.

Pope Paul VI's encyclical *Populorum Progressio* (On the Development of Peoples) in 1967 provided a radical framework and call to action which led, in 1973, to the bishops of Ireland establishing a fund called Trócaire, which means 'mercy', or 'compassion'.

Trócaire was one of a new type of European church organisation, mobilising the laity, which had emerged after the Second Vatican Council, like its sister agencies CAFOD in England and Wales and SCIAF in Scotland. The bishops entrusted Trócaire with a dual mission: to relieve poverty in the developing world, and to raise

Students in an IT class run by the Pallotine Fathers in Arusha, Tanzania   *Lucy Franks*

awareness about the causes of poverty at home here in Ireland. "… Over the first years of its activities," wrote Justin Kilcullen, former Executive Director of Trócaire in book *A Road Less Travelled, Tales of Irish Missionaries.* by A & B Clerkin (Open Air, 2011), "The sense of partnership with the Irish missionary congregations – the Holy Rosary Sisters and the Medical Missionaries of Mary, the Kiltegan Fathers and Columban Fathers and Sisters – became central to Trócaire's development, together with the relationship with so many missionaries from other orders."

Throughout Trócaire's history there is an Irish missionary at the heart of some of the most challenging crises of the late twentieth century: "The struggle to overcome the Marcos dictatorship in the Philippines in the 1980s is marked by the work of the Columban Fathers," Justin continued. "The tremendous efforts made in El Salvador in the late 1970s and 1980s were inspired by the Irish Franciscans … The response to the Ethiopian famine in the mid-1980s was led by the Holy Ghost Fathers … I could go on."

Through working in partnership and in solidarity with Irish missionaries, Trócaire was immediately able to reach the poorest of the poor, and respond to the most urgent needs. This was a mission of mercy to minister to the body of Christ made visible in the suffering of the poor.

This ministry is exemplified in a story that Trócaire's Brazil Project Officer shared with me many years ago: "One day in April 2001, with the Brazilian sun shining warm overhead, I followed Sr. Helen Regan [a Sister of Saint Louis] along the narrow pathway on the side of a hill in the barrio of Perús in the northwest part of the sprawling metropolis of São Paulo, a conurbation of more than 21 million people. We were going to visit one of the women being supported by Bem-me-Quer – an organisation set up by Sr. Helen to help people living with HIV and AIDS. In common with the peripheries of many cities in the developing world, in Perús there is poverty, crime, poor infrastructure, inadequate service provision and a high population density.

"I cannot call the building we came to a house. It was typical of thousands of homes in slums throughout the developing world – a confection of wood and plastic barely eight feet by ten. But, it was someone's home and the woman, let us call her Maria, welcomed Sr. Helen as a dear friend and with a grace that would not have been out of place in a mansion. Inside, the dwelling consisted of one room, long enough to accommodate the single bed that, during the day, was piled high with Maria's belongings in various boxes and bags. Behind a hardboard partition, a toilet bowl was perched precariously over a channel that discharged into the open sewer that ran in front of the shack. Sr. Helen and I sat and talked with Maria for a while and then went on our way.

"I've never forgotten that encounter. The lasting impression that has stayed with me over the years is of Sr. Helen's compassion, and of her affirmation of Maria's inherent human dignity. Sr. Helen passed away in 2011, but the work of Bem-me-Quer continues to bring compassion and support to people living on the margins in São Paulo."

I have encountered many more examples of such compassion, both personally, and in stories from Trócaire staff, of the work of missionary orders and lay missionaries alike, who work in the enormous slums of some of the greatest cities in the developing world, cities like Nairobi, Manila, and Sao Paulo, and in some of the remotest places on the planet, like the Amazonian region of northern Brazil.

In Ireland, the Church is faced with a reality of falling Mass attendance, and a decline in vocations, while the reverse is happening in countries where Irish missionaries have been active for decades. As a wise Spiritan missionary once said, when critiquing the administrative burden of logical frameworks and impact assessments increasingly associated with grant funding, "It is easy to measure the seeds in an apple, but it is harder to measure the apples in a seed." We asked him how organisations like Trócaire can better support his work, and the work of missionaries overseas. He replied that Trócaire was already doing it: by listening, and by having empathy. This is what he needed most when returning to his missionary work: to know that he was being heard.

From the perspective of Catholic Social Teaching, the ongoing work of missionaries gives expression to the principle of subsidiarity and the dignity of the human person. This consistency in building capacity and empowering religious and local communities has made a significant contribution towards the development of the Global South. These are the apple seeds which the Irish missionaries have planted throughout the world. Ultimately, this is their legacy.

Éamonn Meehan is Executive Director of Trócaire.

V

The Impact of Irish Missionaries in Developing Countries
Dr. Eamonn Brehony

"I was a direct beneficiary of Ireland's contribution to the education system in the country" so said President Uhuru Kenyatta of Kenya in 2014 at the presentation of his credentials by Dr. Vincent O Neill, the Irish ambassador to Kenya. President Kenyatta noted that he had been educated by Irish missionaries and he praised the Irish "because for all the time they have been in the country they came to contribute and not to take."

In 2013 Irish Aid carried out an independent review of its funding to Misean Cara to support the development work of Irish missionaries and their partners. That report stated: "Many congregations displayed a high degree of technical competency in the provision of services in education and healthcare, and this is accompanied by a high degree of personal commitment on the part of congregation members and staff." It also noted that many programmes and projects implemented by missionary congregations target poorer, more vulnerable and marginalised sections of society, often providing services that might not otherwise be available to these needy beneficiaries.

Bishop Maurice Crowley of the Catholic Diocese of Kitale in Kenya compliments the Daughters of Charity there because they live among the poor and the marginalised so there is close contact between them as they are part of the local community. This is a unique feature of how missionaries operate.

In the course of my work evaluating various projects I can testify to the impact of the work of many Irish missionaries. When I travel to remote areas in different countries I meet Irish missionaries who are either complementing government services in health or education or working creatively in other areas and closely with local communities.

Missionaries traditionally are known for their high quality service delivery in education and in health. I have worked with Saruji Secondary School in Tanga, Tanzania. It was owned by a company who in 2000 handed it over to the Rosminian Fathers to manage. When the Rosminians took it over, the average mark of the students in Form 2 was 34 points, and the O level results were Division 4 – the lowest division. By 2005 these results had jumped to an average of 79 in Form 2, and O level had achieved Division 2 status. By 2012, it was seventh in the country and it has continued to be in the top 15 schools in the country according to O level results.

In the course of an evaluation I did in Ghana a former Minster for Education there, Osafo Marfo, praised the Sisters of Our Lady of Apostles (OLA) for being pioneers in girls' education in Ghana, and said: "The quality of the work of the OLAs influenced me to give back the management of schools to missions against a lot of opposition."

The same can be said about health care and health service delivery. Missionaries are well known for their health care services – their work in hospitals, health centres and dispensaries. A chief in Ghana told me that "many more of us would have already gone to our ancestors if not for the care we receive in the mission hospital."

In the course of a review of the work of the Medical Missionaries of Mary (MMM) that I did in Nigeria, through using a formula to standardise the various services into one unit of output – the equivalent of seeing one outpatient – we found that the congregation treated half a million outpatients in one year. Apart from their work in service delivery, Irish missionaries have been pioneers in approaches to address specific health issues. Two issues I single out here – addressing the consequences of HIV/AIDS and caring for the elderly and dying.

A HIV/AIDS programme run by the Daughters of Charity in Nairobi, Kenya is rated by the National AIDS and STIs Control Programme (NASCOP) as "one of the best programmes in the country and is a leader in patient care and management." The programme is very professional in the way it engages with the community. For example, it works with groups of discordant couples. When it comes to the issue of one partner making disclosure to the other that he/she is HIV positive, this is a very difficult stage in the evolution of the relationship between couples. A counsellor is always present with the couple to help at the time of disclosure. The couples in the group told me that despite the difficulty of the issue, all the couples in the groups have remained together after disclosure.

The above mentioned HIV/AIDS programme has the ability to elicit great commitment from its community volunteers to visit and support those who are sick at home. One day I accompanied Ann – a home care visitor – on her rounds. Every day at 9am she visits one lady who has AIDS, as she is on medication for TB. This is the second time for the lady to get TB in the last 12 months. It is important that she takes her medication at the same time each day. Ann keeps the TB medication and administers it daily at 9.00am. She walks thirty minutes each day to the home of this lady – the day we went together we were five minutes late and the lady reminded Ann of that fact.

The Daughters of Charity at Thigio in Kenya work with the elderly and the dying. There are three support groups for elderly people, and in the course of a review I found that some elderly walk up to 5km to come to the group. The routine for the day includes tea and then the physiotherapist does physical exercises with them. All the elderly appreciated this activity as they said it helped them 'to loosen out'. They would like to come twice a week as they look forward to the social element as well as the activities.

This congregation also has a hospice. They have a 'visitor's comments book'. An analysis of the comments illustrated the wonderful care that clients received and how they were comfortable and at peace on their final journey. One comment written on 16 March 2015 was: "I wish on behalf of my family to congratulate your hospice for your unique style of hospitality, respect and medical work. Your continued support has been felt in our entire family. Our family will be ambassadors

Irish Ambassador, Vincent O'Neill (centre right) meeting Irish missionaries in Kitale, Kenya

Irish Embassy, Nairobi

of the good work done in your hospice." This sentiment was echoed by the chief nursing officer in Nairobi Hospice Project. She said that this hospice makes a big contribution to Kenya as it offers first class care and service.

As well as delivering quality health and education services, some missionaries have developed innovative ways of engaging with communities. I know two Daughters of Charity in Kenya who have used soccer as a way to positively engage the youth. These sisters have organised soccer leagues during holiday time, and hundreds attend. These leagues have become a gateway to some members playing in higher national leagues. The youth also experience all the positive benefits of sport. Alcohol consumption and smoking marijuana has decreased. Ten members in one club told me that they had given up smoking marijuana. Others received opportunities to study in secondary school which otherwise they would not have received. In 2015, fourteen boys and girls were on scholarships in secondary schools under this scheme.

Another target group that is difficult to reach is ex-brewers. In a poor urban community in Kitale where illicit alcohol brewing is a major problem, the Daughters of Charity have set up a group of ex-brewers – women who meet weekly. They are organised in small groups where they form friendships and focus on saving money which is then lent out to members and can be used in enterprising ways.

The Sisters of the Sacred Hearts of Jesus and Mary (SSHJM) were working in Mbala District in Zambia to change the attitude of a community dependent on external support. A review of this programme showed that 74 homes with orphan and vulnerable children (OVC), who were originally dependent on support from the programme, are now able to take responsibility for their own lives and the lives of their families.

One of the 74 is Mwenzi Nkumbwa. She is 41 years old and is caring for orphans who were getting support from the programme. Through that support, she became involved in agriculture. She received fertiliser and advice. In the first year she harvested 1,500kg of maize. The following year she harvested 1,700kg of maize. She used five bags for household needs and sold the rest. She is now able to feed and clothe her children and she has bought a plot of land, and plants vegetables – rapeseed and pumpkin. She is now independent with a sustainable livelihood.

In the course of my work I have met with many government officials in various African countries. Generally, they are very appreciative and complementary on the work of missionaries. In a recent evaluation of a programme in Zambia, an Acting District Commissioner commended the work of the SSHJM sisters. This congregation was, among other things, working with children and youth with special needs. The Commissioner told me, "This congregation had provided a wakeup call for the government by providing services for people with special needs as the government had gone to sleep on special needs in this district and this project has been able to identify children with multiple special needs and to support them." The town clerk also praised this congregation for working in places where government does not have the capacity to deliver services.

These examples of missionary work show the positive impact that many missionaries have, based on my personal engagement with some of them. However, many missionary projects are likely to be cost-effective, and may be producing good development outcomes, but it is often not possible to confirm these outcomes because of the lack of proper results management systems. Perhaps missionaries need to listen more carefully to the words of St. Matthew in his gospel when he reminds us that people do not light a lamp and put it under a bowl. Instead they put it on its stand, and it gives light to everyone in the house. In the same way, let your light shine before others that they may see your good deeds and glorify your Father in heaven (Matthew 5:15-16).

Dr. Eamonn Brehony is an international development consultant based in Tanzania. With a Ph.D in culture and development, he has worked for 27 years as field officer and programme manager with the Spiritan Congregation in Gambia, with Concern in Tanzania, Uganda, Sudan and Ethiopia, with Irish Aid in Tanzania, and currently with the Medical Missionaries of Mary in Tanzania.

VI

Distinctive Features of the Irish Missionary Movement

Delivering the opening address to the *Mission Today and Tomorrow Conference*, Nigerian-born, Fr. Agbonkhianmeghe Orobator, then Provincial of the Eastern Africa Province of the Society of Jesus reminded delegates, "Wherever you look, in Africa, Asia, the Pacific, South America and the West Indies, Irish missionaries – sisters, priests, brothers, lay volunteers and lay missionaries – have bestrode the globe like the Shakespearean colossus as vanguards of the good news of Jesus Christ."

Commending the agenda of the Irish missionaries he said: "In some parts of Africa, the advent of Christianity is almost always associated with the establishment of western colonial political hegemony and economic exploitation. However, unlike the French, English, Portuguese, Spanish, Dutch, Belgian, and Italian, Irish missionaries had the unique distinction of not fronting the hegemonic agenda of a colonising power. Although former President Mary McAleese famously eulogised them as unpaid ambassadors of Ireland, they avoided overt political and economic interests that so often cast missionary endeavours in the shadow of an ambiguous adventure."

He also noted the uniquely inclusive nature of the movement. "Ireland's brand of missionary Christianity was an example of inclusive ecclesial mission in terms of its composition. The missionary caravan of priests, sisters and brothers came from various and diverse religious congregations, but it also included diocesan priests, members of societies of apostolic life, and a significant number of lay people," he pointed out.

Fr. Orobator illustrated how "women played a vital role in the missionary economy. Ubiquitous and heroic communities of women religious and members of societies of apostolic life defied unimaginable odds to establish and manage educational and healthcare institutions in several parts of sub-Saharan Africa, while providing pastoral support in parishes and remote outstations" he concluded.

Those educational and healthcare institutions became the nucleus of the development work of the Irish missionaries. In December 2006 international consultants engaged by IMRS to analyse the organisational capacity within a number of congregations for managing development interventions reported: "The review teams were impressed by the relevance, quality and range of the development work. Without exception, the congregations contribute very considerable 'added value' to what they receive from their respective external donor partners, in terms of their long-term commitment to host communities, credibility with the local people, and conferring real value for money."

They concluded: "Their track record in working with the poor and most disadvantaged, their combination of caring and professionalism, their long-term commitment, their ability to raise funds from a wide range of sources and their cost-effectiveness are models of development work."

In a book – *The Irish Legacy: a Story of the Irish Contribution to Education in India* – commissioned by the Irish Embassy in New Delhi, and published by Amber Books in 2012, the distinctive impact made by Irish missionaries in India was described thus (page 17): "The magnitude of the impact of Irish Catholic missions on India and Indians is impossible to quantify. It becomes even more difficult in the overall context of Irish Catholic missions in other parts of the Christian world ... the Irish missionaries in India were to irrevocably influence successive generations of young Indians ... they negotiated their way around social taboos and barriers of class and creed to create a milieu where children could connect without the debilitating constraints of religion or caste. This harmonious interaction would bridge long-standing divides and build relationships that went beyond familial canons or communal indoctrination ..."

Holy Rosary Sisters Mary Mullin, Ann Kelly and Bridget Lacey meeting President Ellen Johnson in Liberia – the first woman president of an African state   *Holy Rosary Sisters*

Chapter Two

The Dedication of Irish Missionaries

As the Great Famine hit Ireland in 1845, four Loreto Sisters left Dublin aboard a cargo boat – *The Reaper* – bound for Mauritius, and took three months to arrive there. One of the sisters, Sr. Camilla MacCormick, wrote on 4 June about their departure from Loreto Abbey, Rathfarnham saying: "It was with great difficulty we tore ourselves from our peaceful happy home. But as we have generously made the sacrifice for the love of God, so for that same love, will we courageously proceed to labour and await our recompense in heaven where I trust we shall all meet, never more to separate."

So many early missionaries found themselves in similar situations, but their faith and love of God and their personal dedication to help others drove them on whilst knowing that they were not likely to return to their loved ones in Ireland.

A report by an Irish Aid consultant reviewing Misean Cara in 2007 stated: "During the visit to Kenya we came upon many exceptional individuals, of many nationalities, often working in very difficult conditions with extraordinary dedication, and achieving visible impacts for the people with whom they were working."

That is a familiar description of the work of missionaries. In this chapter a number of well-placed individuals describe their personal experiences of witnessing and analysing the contribution of Irish missionaries in the Global South.

Missionaries are a Beacon of Hope and Excellence
Professor Stephen Morse

Few would deny that Sierra Leone has had a tortuous – and tortured – past. The outbreak of the Ebola virus in 2014 features large in recent memory. The country has experienced a difficult historical legacy, both as a British protectorate and colony, and since independence in 1961. In spite of being well-endowed with minerals, the country has suffered dramatic economic decline and political instability since the mid-1980s. Sierra Leone experienced five military coups between 1967 and 1991, and a 10-year civil conflict from 1991 to 2002, characterised by mass killings, sexual violence and the use of child soldiers.

Hospitals and schools became targets of attack and many had to be vacated. Thousands of people lost their lives and hundreds of thousands were forced from their homes, some becoming internally displaced persons, others fleeing to neighbouring Guinea as refugees.

Sierra Leone is mainly rural. It is estimated that seventy percent live in absolute poverty and life expectancy at birth is estimated at 56 years. Current estimates of the adult literacy rate are 58% for men and 37% for women.

Yet the enigma that is Sierra Leone reveals many positive features. It is regarded as one of the most religiously tolerant nations. Muslims and Christians collaborate and interact with each other peacefully. Religious violence is very rare in the country.

The Missionary Sisters of the Holy Rosary (MSHR), which was founded in Ireland, but is now nationally diverse, came to Sierra Leone in 1948 at the invitation of Bishop Ambrose Kelly CSSp, then Bishop of Freetown and Bo. They established a presence in Freetown, the capital of Sierra Leone, and in the southern towns of Kenema, Bo, Pujehun and then further afield, working to bring education especially to women, and provide health care to mothers, children and the population in general.

During the bitter civil war, MSHRs helped the many refugees in need of protection with the means of bare survival. Many had been subjected to brutality and maiming. When the war ended, there began the long and arduous task of building life anew and re-opening schools and hospitals – a work still in progress. The raw legacy of conflict and the moral, social and psychological aftershock, coupled with drug abuse, created a great need for counselling, trauma release and healing management.

MSHRs stepped into the breach as soon as the war ended in a very practical manner: Sisters pursued qualifications in group dynamics, group counselling and one-to-one counselling, so as to facilitate community outreach training in a range of 'hard' and 'soft' skills, including inter-personal communication, counselling, income generation and dealing with domestic conflict. Innovation and self-confidence gradually grew among these refugees – young women and men – who had lost so much and endured levels of persecution and insecurity that are almost unimaginable.

While the need for healing still continues, MSHRs have in recent years advanced into pastures new in Sierra Leone by promoting and supporting work in agriculture. This makes sense given that over 60% of the population is rural, that food security is a high national priority and that only between 11% and 15% of Sierra Leone's arable land is cultivated. Indeed before the civil war, Sierra Leone led Africa in agricultural research.

The potential of the agricultural sector is obvious with vast areas of available land and a large proportion of Sierra Leoneans working in agriculture. The smallholder is central to the government's commercialisation of agriculture policy and action programme. This involves moving small farmers from household subsistence to running their farms as a business, thereby increasing both food self-sufficiency and incomes for the most vulnerable.

I have been involved in projects with MSHRs for many years and co-published several books and journal articles with Sr. Nora McNamara who was until recently their development officer. To help strengthen their agricultural outreach, I was invited in 2014 to help them in the establishment of a new farm run by the Catholic Women's Association (CWA), a group of 150 women who advocate, "Love for each other and consideration for others."

The initiative is led by Sr. Bernadette Ezeabasili, a Nigerian MSHR. For MSHRs, it signifies the continuing move from being primarily relief-centred to being more development orientated. The farm occupies prime land favourably located near to Bo. The land title was a gift to the CWA from the Paramount Chief (a scientist who for many years taught in MSHR's Queen of the Rosary Secondary School in Bo), with encouragement of the Bishop of Bo, Dr. Charles Campbell. Both share the hope that what these sisters did for women in education can now be done for women in agriculture.

In their commitment to agriculture in Sierra Leone, MSHRs were able to build on their extensive work in this sector elsewhere in West Africa. This facilitates a sharing of knowledge and insights born out of diverse experience in conditions that encourage maximum participation.

This initiative is but one example of the competence being shown by MSHRs in Sierra Leone. Their work, enthusiasm and dedication are impressive – a true beacon of hope and excellence in a place that so badly needs it. They represent all that is commendable in the body of Irish missionaries who devoted their lives to the disadvantaged. Their achievements in Sierra Leone are a tangible representation of a tremendous legacy that is now being carried forward by local sisters from Sierra Leone and other African countries. It is also an example of the carrying forward of the legacy by thousands of missionaries in other congregations.

Prof. Stephen Morse is Chair of Systems Analysis for Sustainability, Centre for Environmental Strategy in University of Surrey. He has authored and co-authored several books, and been involved in research and sustainable projects across continents. His research interests include partnerships in sustainable development, including the role of faith-inspired groups.

II

The Contribution of Irish Missionaries in Uganda
Professor Charles Olweny

There are two social services that are the purview of government. These are health and education. In Uganda, Christian churches spear-headed the development of these services. At the request of Bishop Henry Hanlon, Teresa Kearney, better known as Mother Kevin, arrived in Uganda in January 1903. She is the founder of two religious congregations – the Little Sisters of St. Francis of Assisi (LSoSF) in Uganda and the Franciscan Missionary Sisters for Africa (FMSA) in Ireland. Soon after her arrival she established a 'clinic under a mango tree' which was later to convert into St. Francis Hospital, Nsambya.

Nsambya Hospital is now the largest Catholic hospital in Uganda with a capacity of 361 beds. It became affiliated with Uganda Martyrs University in 2010 to provide

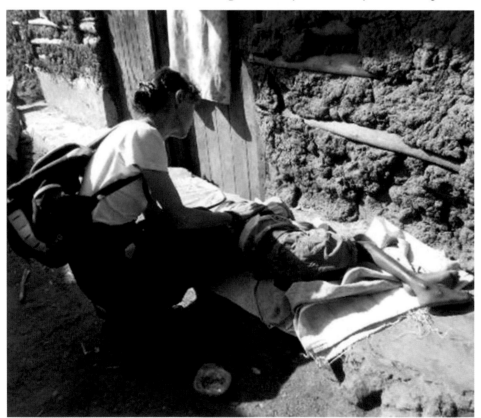

Sr. Patricia Speight FMSA attending to a sick child in a slum in Nukuru, Kenya

Love and Hope Centre, Nukuru

post graduate medical education, and has so far seen three cohorts graduate with Master of Medicine degrees. In 1906, the Franciscan Missionary Sisters for Africa established another hospital at Naggalama in Mukono District which now has 100 beds. Both Nsambya and Naggalama hospitals are general hospitals. The Franciscan sisters developed special institutions in Nyenga and Buloba to specifically cater for leprosy patients.

As for education provided by the sisters, one institution that stands out is Mount St. Mary's at Namagunga founded in 1942 and now has an enrolment of about 1,000 students. Many of the top-notch females in Uganda received their secondary education in Namagunga. The ones that come to mind are Dr. Josephine Nambooze the first female medical doctor in East and Central Africa. She graduated in 1959, and is now Professor Emeritus in Public Health at Makerere University. Another who comes to mind is Dr. Specioza Kazibwe the first female Vice President of Uganda. Then, we have Ms. Winnie Byanyima, an aeronautical engineer, and Professor Mary Okwakol who is currently Vice Chancellor of Busitema University.

The Nursing School started in 1919 with 12 midwifery students. Today, the school has over 700 students comprising registered nurses and midwives, enrolled nurses and midwives, laboratory technicians and technologists. Plans are ready to activate a B.Sc. programme in nursing and midwifery in the next academic year.

I have been associated with the Franciscan Missionary Sisters for Africa and continue to interact with the LSoSF. In 1944, I joined St. Maria Gorretti Primary School that was founded in 1931. My late elder sister trained as an enrolled nurse at Nsambya Hospital in 1952. In 1975, I was invited by Archbishop Emmanuel Nsubuga (later His Eminence Emmanuel Cardinal Nsubuga) to chair the first Board of Governors of the hospital. Sr. Miriam Duggan, later Superior General of the Franciscan Missionary Sisters, was on this first board. I held this position until 1982.

After my return in 2006, I was requested by Archbishop Cyprian Kizito Lwanga to take over again as board chairman, and have served three terms. I am happy to have been involved with the Franciscan Missionary Sisters as well as with the LSoSF – two congregations who have contributed so much to services in health and education in Uganda.

Prof. Charles Olweny is a Ugandan physician, oncologist, academic and medical researcher. He served as Vice Chancellor of Uganda Martyrs University, as President of the Uganda Medical Association, and as Director of the Uganda Cancer Institute.

III
For Missionaries, Working with the Poor is not a Job – it is a Way of Life
Mags Gargan

Long before Ireland had an official aid programme, Irish missionaries were the frontier men and women of international development. Their journeys into the unknown pre-dated the internet, cheap air fares and even television, which have all contributed to making the world a smaller and more familiar place today.

I have often marvelled at the courage it must have taken to leave a small town in rural Ireland for the first time for formation training and then find yourself on a boat travelling to Africa, Asia or South America, knowing little of what to expect when you got there. Or the patience and tenacity it must have taken to grow a mission from those humble beginnings to building a school or a hospital, which still stands today serving the community.

I always had a vague idea of the good work done 'on the missions' thanks to school fundraising projects or parish collections. I saw missionaries as nice older priests and religious who collected money for the world's poor. However, it wasn't until I began to interview missionaries and to hear their amazing stories first-hand that I began to appreciate how incredible their work is. One of my first interviews was a sister who worked with aborigines in Australia's outback, travelling to remote places while living and working out of the back of a truck. This was when I realised that they were true pioneers and innovators.

It is notoriously difficult to get missionaries to talk about themselves. They are a humble lot – unfussy, practical-minded and focused on their work. But I think missionary congregations and societies are now realising the importance of capturing missionary stories and creating a history of what has been achieved.

I was once asked what is it that made missionaries different from other people working in development. My first thought was that missionaries were there first. But there is also the fact that they are often there last – they are last to evacuate when things become dangerous. However, it is more than that. For missionaries, working with the poor and marginalised is not a job – it is a way of life. They live side-by-side with the people they support, building relationships and trust, experiencing their hardships and needs.

A few years ago I had the privilege of staying with a Presentation sister living in a shanty town outside Peru's capital of Lima. There we walked the dusty streets, everyday visiting shacks, where a project she founded – organised and carried out by locals – was installing plumbed bathrooms at an affordable price.

Four Irish Presentation sisters moved there in 1998 to live in their own simple wooden house. Struggling up the dusty hillsides with buckets of water from delivery trucks in the searing heat of the summer, to sliding through the mud caused by the constant mists of winter, the sisters campaigned side-by-side with their neighbours to gain access to basic services like water, sanitation and electricity. This is the real strength of missionaries – they can see the needs of the community because they are members of the community too.

The sisters inspired community leaders to become agents of change by showing them how to advocate and to negotiate with the authorities, how to establish community projects and, ultimately, how to be self-sufficient. They inspired confidence and built the capacity of community leaders.

Most missionaries will tell you that their role is to put themselves out of a job. They empower local people so that they can take over and continue a project. Many young local missionaries are continuing the work of Irish missionaries, and along with lay Irish missionaries, they are the successors of those original pioneers. While the profile of missionaries may be changing, the legacy of their work continues to bear fruit for the poor and deprived.

Mags Gargan is Features Editor of The Irish Catholic newspaper where she has interviewed many missionaries. She edited the report on the Mission Today & Tomorrow Conference.

An income generation project at the KUAP – Pandipieri Centre in Kisumu, Kenya   *Lucy Franks*

IV
Missionaries are Held in Very High Regard by Their Communities
Brian Kenny

My experience meeting Irish Columbans in Myanmar was much like my experience when I made an earlier documentary on them in the Philippines. They were held in very high regard by their communities through both personal experiences of individuals whom I met and through children of those who remember the Columbans. Obviously from a historical perspective the Columbans have had a huge impact in Myanmar, particularly with the Kachin people who came to respect the Irish missionaries for their authenticity and in particular for how they lived with the people on a day-to-day basis. Many of the Kachins mentioned to me how their traditional spiritual practices were respected by the Columbans which was not the case with previous missionaries.

In an educational capacity the Columbans played an important role wherever they went, but particularly here where there was such a dire need. There were many stories about the Columbans who were interned during the war and how many of them sacrificed themselves in solidarity with the Kachins.

The Columban Sisters' presence is more recent, but their current work is inspirational. Starting from modest beginnings they now deal with a huge number of problems in and around the internally displaced people during the ongoing conflict between the Kachin and state forces. I visited the HOPE Centre and Clay Centre and saw first-hand how they indiscriminately help drug addicts and HIV patients regardless of religion or race. As Sr. Mary Dillon put it herself, "They leave their war and differences outside, it's not welcome here, this is a place of peace and healing."

In recent times the Columban Fathers have started a new project in Myanmar through Fr. Neil Magill. I visited his education project nostalgically located in the old building where the Columbans were interned during World War II, and saw how he is enthusiastically, against all odds, reaching out to the youth and pushing education forward.

My lasting impression of their work is that it stays true to their motto of working at grassroots level with the people and most of all, unlike most Irish peoples' impressions of missionaries as elderly priests converting the poor; they are involved in working where the need lies, in this instance education and health.

I met two young indigenous priests who were educated by the Columbans and are continuing on the work of the earlier Columbans. Two of the sisters working with Sr. Mary Dillon in Myitichyina are from South Korea.

I met with a group of Xaverian sisters who were educated by the Columban Sisters in Myanmar. They told me about many of their friends and family members who only got an education because of the Columban Sisters, and they are now working in successful careers. I met with two young men from Myanmar who are studying to be Columban priests and are hoping to continue the work of the Columbans to "give back to the people" as they put it. This is in line with my experience of the continuation of the legacy of the Columbans in other parts of the world.

Brian Kenny is a documentary maker who produced "The Kachin Hills" featuring Columban priests and sisters in Myanmar, and was broadcast on Newstalk radio in Ireland on 31 January 2015. He also produced "Remembering Rufus" which was broadcast on Newstalk on 13 November 2013.

V

Missionary Zeal: Ireland's Informal Diplomatic Corps
Joe Humphreys

Missionaries have done the state some service. For part of the last century they acted as an informal diplomatic corps for the newly independent Irish Republic; in more recent years they played a pivotal role in shaping the State's overseas development policy and in giving birth to a number of national and international aid agencies, as well as spawning a still-vibrant volunteering tradition in Ireland.

Missionaries also greatly enhanced Ireland's international reputation, something that continues to have practical benefits today. The telecoms tycoon, Denis O'Brien, for example, describes missionaries as "advance point people" for Irish companies trying to break into emerging markets. The advantages are heightened where members of the local political and business elite went through Irish mission schools.

"We got most of our licences in the Caribbean because we were Irish," says O'Brien. While Ireland's artistic or cultural heritage might open doors in the United States, he says: "If you take these [developing] countries, they have never heard of Seamus Heaney. So it's really because of the work of missionaries who have effectively created unbelievable goodwill towards Ireland."

Calculating the impact of the movement is tricky. You can cite success stories like the Kenyan environmentalist Wangari Maathai, the first African woman to win the Nobel Peace Prize, who credits Irish Loreto Sisters with unlocking her passion for both science and social justice. "After my education by the nuns," she says, "I emerged as a person who believed that society is inherently good and that people generally act for the best."

Or you can estimate the contribution of individual missionaries, such as Sr. Cyril Mooney, a Co Wicklow native whom the Indian government has credited with helping up to 450,000 people during her time in Kolkata, where she now runs education, nutrition and micro-finance schemes.

But, however you do the maths, you can only conclude that the legacy of the missionary movement is significant. In fact, it is hard to identify a cultural phenomenon emanating from the state that has had such a profound international impact.

Joe Humphreys is Assistant News Editor with the Irish Times, author of 'God's Entrepreneurs: how Irish missionaries tried to change the world', and a number of other books. He has worked as a reporter in South Africa, and has a particular interest in development issues.

VI
Remarkable Priests and Nuns doing Remarkable Things

Writing in *The Irish Catholic* on 19 March 2010, Tom Arnold, then Chief Executive of Concern Worldwide noted: "The Irish missionary tradition has made a signal contribution, maintained over many decades, in delivering education, improving health and promoting human development for hundreds of millions of poor people."

He continued: "Religion must continue to bear witness against injustice. Much of the world's extreme poverty is rooted in discrimination against minorities. Religious leaders have a key role in articulating their basic values and in maintaining an appropriate distance from state power, especially if that power is perpetuating injustice and oppression.

"Religions must be fully co-opted into the agenda for development of peoples. Over the past 60 years, core principles from the great religions have underpinned the evolving language and conventions of human rights and the codes of conduct for humanitarian action. These provide the common ground for religious institutions and humanitarian non-denominational organisations, such as Concern and many others, to cooperate," he concluded.

Irish broadcaster and journalist, Charlie Bird, travelled to the Philippines and South Korea in June 2015 for World Missions Ireland to record a video on the work of missionaries there. At the launch of the video in Dublin on 6 October

Matt Moran, then Chairman of Misean Cara, planting a tree as a symbol of growth and renewal at the KUAP - Pandipieri Centre at Kisumu, Kenya in 2014   *Lucy Franks*

2015, he reflected on his admiration for the work and solidarity of missionaries with their chosen communities: "Like many institutions in Ireland over the past few decades, the Catholic Church has had its difficulties – but none of that should take away from the excellent work which the missionaries continue to do while working abroad," he said. "As a reporter in RTÉ, in many places where I went I met remarkable missionary priests and nuns doing remarkable things, and they did it away from the glare of publicity, away from their families and their homes. If people in Ireland had the opportunity like I had to meet them, they too would surely be proud of them."

The President of Ireland, Michael D. Higgins when presenting a Presidential Distinguished Service Award on 3 December 2015 to Sr. Miriam Duggan – a member of the Franciscan Missionary Sisters for Africa – remarked: "Sr. Dr. Miriam Duggan's tireless medico-humanitarian work on the African continent across the fields of midwifery and the care of those afflicted by HIV/AIDS represents one of the most impressive examples of Irish diasporic empathy in practice."

"The missionaries have made a tremendous contribution to education and health in Tanzania," Anne Barrington, Irish Ambassador to that country told the *UCD Connections* alumni magazine in 2009. Her view represents that of most ambassadors who have served in developing countries where they witnessed missionary work.

Writing in *The Irish Catholic* after spending some time with Irish Spiritans in Brazil in 2012, journalist Cathal Barry stated: "From what I have witnessed during my time in São Paulo, the Irish Spiritans have an unrivalled ability to engage lay people in active ministry within the church and to animate young people in such a way that they are not merely products of mission but become agents of mission themselves. It was an exceptional privilege to witness first hand the phenomenal contribution of the Irish Spiritans, not only to the building up of the church in Brazil, but to the lives of so many of the country's poorest as well."

In 2013 Dr. Monique Oliff of Wellsense Public Health Consultancy reviewed health projects in Kenya that had been grant aided by Misean Cara. In her report she stated: "Overall the quality of the care and patient interaction across the projects was excellent, standards of care exceed that of public facilities, and projects were committed to achieving the objectives set out for Misean Cara and their other donors. The Misean Cara members reach a substantial number of Kenyans requiring health care and they do so with a remarkable commitment to social justice and the needs of the poorest and most underprivileged. The members also demonstrate resilience to funding uncertainties and commitment to the long term development of their beneficiaries. Through further support, partnerships and exchange these projects can continue to provide critical services to communities who are not reached by others."

VII
The Lasting Impact of One Irish Missionary on a Rural Community in Nigeria
Dr. Utiang Ugbe

I first came in contact with Irish nun, Sr. Nora McNamara, and began collaborating with her important work in Nigeria when my company served as the local implementing partner for the *Agricultural Research into Use Programme* – an important agricultural project centrally funded by United Kingdom's Department for International Development. Under the terms of collaboration, Sr. Nora initiated and successfully drove, through the management structure of a Catholic Diocesan community outreach, a rural enterprise development project focusing on the production of seed yams.

An understanding of the context in which Sr. Nora's pioneering work was done is important to a proper appreciation of the enormity of her achievements. Yam is a major staple food in today's Nigeria, akin to what the potato was to Ireland in the 19th century. Farming operations are still mostly manually carried out, requiring tedious manual labour. Furthermore, although most yam farming is for subsistence, about 50% of the harvest must be preserved as seed for the subsequent farming season, thereby leaving only about one-half of the entire harvest for use by the farming family. Normally, in this scenario, most yam farmers cannot have any tubers left for sale in order to generate much-needed household income to meet other pressing basic needs. Any yam-farming family that eats all of its stored yams effectively eats its seed resources for the next planting season.

To address these issues, Sr. Nora initiated a suitable enterprise model for seed yam multiplication, successfully demonstrated the profitability of the model, and promoted the model's uptake among rural yam farmers in target zones in Nigeria. The entrepreneurial success of the model was evidenced by the financial profits earned by the participating farmers, and an increase in the supply of seed yams to farmers at affordable prices.

By enabling some yam farmers to specialise in the production of seed yams, their farm sizes and total yam output increased four-fold, while lowering their average total costs. Consequently, the participating farmers could sell at affordable prices and still make a profit. The availability of seed yams at affordable prices removed the need for yam farmers to set aside 50% of their yam harvest for use as seed in the subsequent planting season. This effectively freed up what would have been reserved as seed, allowing the farming families to have 50% more yams than they previously could. Yam-farming households could then use more of the yams as food, or sell them in the local market for much-needed income, knowing that they could acquire new seed yams at affordable prices when the next planting season comes.

The success of Sr. Nora's rural-based pilot project on seed yam multiplication gave rise, within a few years, to a major program funded by the Bill & Melinda Gates Foundation, enabling the International Institute of Tropical Agriculture (IITA) to deepen the scientific aspects of seed yam breeding and multiplication, and extend the technology and enterprise model to farmers across Nigeria and West Africa. It effectively increased the interaction between the research scientists and the users of agricultural research.

Her work demonstrated the importance of embedding agricultural research within the sphere of economic application, thereby giving recognition to the farmers as dignified partners in the value chain, rather than treating them as ignorant people to be talked down to and told what to do and how to do it. Sr. Nora's work proved effective in building the capacity of the local farmers, and enabling them to imbibe entrepreneurial sense, thereby integrating a business approach to their subsistence farming.

I have talked with some of the yam farmers who participated in the seed yam multiplication training and enterprise model led by Sr. Nora, and each of them has told me that they are now thriving seed yam entrepreneurs. Some have afforded new houses, or new means of transportation, or school fees for their children – all things that were once out of reach to them.

The scope of Sr. Nora's work in local economic development in Nigeria is much wider than just yam multiplication. For example, she initiated and successfully implemented a rural micro-credit (savings and loans) facility among low-income women in 1973, only 2 years after the Nigerian (Biafran) civil war – one of the first such facilities in post-colonial Africa.

Sr. Nora's work in local economic development has empowered lives and freed people from the bondage of poverty. To the thousands of people whose lives have been profoundly enhanced by her work, she is a true hero and a great ambassador of Ireland.

Dr. Utiang P. Ugbe is the founder and CEO of Development Input Ltd., an economic development consulting firm based in Abuja, Nigeria

This case history illustrates the professionalism and transformative change that one missionary brought about collaboratively in a deprived region and in an era when the practice of international development was only emerging. That type of community impact can be illustrated by many other projects and programmes undertaken by other missionaries across sectors amongst poor and deprived communities. Many of these pioneering individuals have been recognised with awards for their contribution by the governments of their host countries including South Africa, Zambia, Sierra Leone, Uganda, Singapore, South Korea, Japan, India, St. Lucia and by the Council of Europe. Many others have been recognised by universities and other such institutes. However, missionaries neither work for nor seek praise or glory for their efforts for their brothers and sisters in Christ. They avoid self-aggrandisement. Their work is not a job; it is a vocation in every sense.

VIII
"Thanks to your Noble Shadow"

Irish-born journalist, James Creedon, Media Editor with *MediaWatch* on *France 24* recorded the documentary entitled *Thanks to your Noble Shadow*. The film is about Ireland's last missionary nun in Japan, Sr. Paschal, who was born Jennie O'Sullivan in Co. Cork. It is an emotional and inspiring story about a remarkable missionary, and will become a significant piece of the history of the Irish missionary movement. Here, James describes Sr. Paschal of the Infant Jesus Sisters and her work.

"As someone from another generation who is not a practicing Catholic, I became increasingly curious about what it was that had given Sr. Paschal such strength, joy and luminescence at such an advanced age. At over 100 years old, she was sitting in obscurity in a nursing home in Cork receiving daily letters and cards from her legion of hundreds of adoring past pupils. She genuinely considered her role as English teacher for over 75 years in Japan as being an opportunity to provide motherly love for a vast brood.

"The values and the love she had learned about as a child in Ireland through her family, her community and undoubtedly through her religious practice was then disseminated and discharged consistently over decades – the beneficiaries of this love and charity being generations of Japanese girls who went through her classrooms from 1935 up to 2010. As a cousin 70 years her junior, I was so struck

Fr. James Mannix MSC greeting President Mary McAleese and her husband, Martin, during the President's visit to the MSC community in Cork in 2009 to celebrate their centenary in Ireland

Mike English Photography

by this inner strength and joy when she eventually returned to Ireland at almost 100 years old. It seemed clear to me that through a life of living good acts and kindness and thinking good thoughts – prayerful thoughts if you will – that she had become sublimated. She had reached the apotheosis of our human condition."

The parents, families and friends of the many thousands of Irish missionaries are part of their noble shadow too amongst the poor they chose to serve in the developing world. It is a very noble shadow indeed.

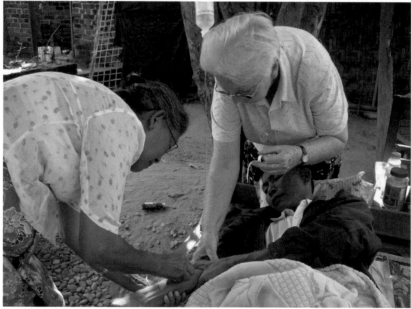

Sr. Mary Dillon SSC attending to the sick in Myanmar   *Columban Sisters*

Chapter Three

Recognition of the Work of Irish Missionaries

"We have left a mark throughout the world through our missionaries, leaving an image of a society that did care," said Peter Sutherland, Special Representative of the UN Secretary General for Migration and Development, and former EU Commissioner when delivering a Trócaire lecture in St. Patrick's College, Maynooth on 19 May 2016.

That "mark" is well recognised globally as Aidan and Brendan Clerkin in their book, *A Road Less Travelled* (Four Courts Press, 2011, page 19), stated: "Go today to various parts of Asia, to Oceania, to South America, to the Caribbean, to North America, and to Africa, and many communities will tell you of the leadership offered by generations of Irish missionaries. People there have long and grateful memories of those who came from afar as young men and women and who stayed for decades enriching deprived communities with their life-long commitment, service and skills. Such people have bequeathed an enduring legacy, not just in passing on their faith, but in invaluable humanitarian and development successes."

Cardinal Ricardo Vidal, Archbishop of Cebu in an interview with Dr. Vincent McKee, Professor of Government at the Catholic University of Manila and published

Sr. Nora McNamara MSHR with farmers in Amoke, West Benue, Nigeria who were involved in the Adopted Yam Mini Sett Technique funded by the Gates Foundation in 2015   *Ada Gabriel*

in *The Irish Catholic* newspaper on 23 December 2004, praised the patient labours of Irish missionaries over the previous 100 years working with the poorest and most deprived peoples in his country. He mentioned in particular the Redemptorists for their Cebu city mission – "an exceptional force for evangelisation" – and the Presentation Sisters "whose ministry to marginalised groups like indigenous peoples, was essential to their well-being."

"Then," he said "there are the Columbans whom I admire as much for their principled stand on human rights and social justice as those many impoverished rural parishes to which they ministered for over 50 years since arriving here after fleeing persecution in Mao's China of the 1950s."

Perhaps mindful of the late Fr. Niall O'Brien SSC – champion of sugar workers from Negros island whose imprisonment during the Marcos era aroused worldwide attention – and Fr. Rufus Halley SSC murdered in 2001 after three decades of peace work among Catholics and Muslims, he commented: "Those Columbans are exceptional for their courage and dedication; they live the gospel as their daily ministry, and we Filipinos owe them a great debt."

His views were echoed by Cardinal Luis Antonio Tagle, Archbishop of Manila in an interview with Mags Gargan in *The Irish Catholic* on 26 May 2016. Referring to the Columban priests he said: "They were always caring pastorally for the poor and the indigenous ethnic communities … these are the images of the Irish missionaries that we have – dedicated, immersed in the realities of the poor and the neglected, and willing to suffer … We are very blessed to have had the witness of them." Cardinal Tagle is current president of Caritas International.

Missionaries serve in a country to give, not to take in any material sense. The Apostolic Nuncio in Trinidad, Archbishop Gullickson, speaking on the occasion of the 175th anniversary of the arrival of the Sisters of St. Joseph of Cluny in the West Indies remarked: "Others came primarily to till the soil and capitalise on this land's natural resources; you came, significantly, to till the hearts and minds of the women and girls of this land, thereby yielding by your love and sacrifices a fruitful harvest for eternity." Quoting the archbishop in her address to the *Mission Today & Tomorrow Conference*, Sr. Clare Stanley SJC from Sierra Leone said: "These words can be applied equally to Irish missionaries in Africa. Only God can measure the contribution Ireland made through its missionaries, women and men, to development in Africa."

Most Rev. Dom Sergio Eduardo Castriali, Archbishop of Manaus in Brazil recognises the legacy of Irish Spiritan priests in his country. "The contribution and mark of the Irish Spiritans in Brazil can be seen very clearly through their work in the shanty towns, through their formation of young leaders in communities, their construction of parishes and their help in building up the local church," he says.

Fr. Jose Altevir Da Silva, Brazilian Superior of the Spiritans agrees with that view. "The greatest contribution of the Irish Spiritans to the church in Brazil has been the diverse lines of missionary works that they became involved in through their preferential option for the poor. The very fact that they are remembered so fondly makes it clear their presence was very important and remains so to this day" he told Cathal Barry of *The Irish Catholic* in an interview in November 2013.

The message is the same in Nigeria where Cardinal Francis Arinze marking the 50th anniversary of his ordination as a bishop gave an interview to Vatican Radio's English Africa Service on 29 August 2015. Speaking about the healthy state of the Catholic Church in Nigeria, he commended the Irish missionaries who were among the earliest in Nigeria.

"Another explanation is the good work done by the missionaries especially the Irish missionaries," he said. "The Irish were very methodical. They promoted good catechetical sacramental preparation and they attended to families. We very much thank God for the local people's response; the first catechists who were near the missionaries; those who gave missionaries land and helped them with the local languages and then the first priests and the religious and the first bishops and the present ones, lay people and families... I believe for all these reasons, the Church in the country is rather strong," he said.

Ugandan priest, Fr. Severinus Ndugwa, spoke at an Irish Aid organised discussion in Dublin in May 2011 on the contribution of Irish missionaries overseas. He referred to the role of the Legion of Mary in Uganda and particularly the example of lay missionary, Edel Quinn, in giving up her homeland to travel to Africa. He pointed out that Irish missionaries had played a role in preserving local languages and culture through the creation of dictionaries in partnership with the people, and a canon of written literature in those languages.

Addressing a question about Irish missionaries' undermining of indigenous culture, Fr. Ndugwa said there were positives as well as negatives. He cited missionaries' contribution to bringing about formal education for girls as, "promoting the position of women in society," and highlighted that the first and only woman vice president of Uganda "is a fruit of Irish labours in the schools they founded." He said: "Irish missionaries had played a role in changing marriage customs such as polygamy, parents marrying off their underage daughters, and in denouncing female genital mutilation in some cultures."

President Michael D. Higgins told the AGM of Misean Cara on 27 May 2015: "While their work was grounded in the Christian values of respect, dignity, compassion, integrity and commitment to the poor, they fitted well into the mores and beliefs of their host communities with their ancient cultures. In recent times during our official visits to countries where Irish missionaries and NGOs are working, Sabina and I have been greatly struck by the solidarity and sense of community developed by missionaries through their practical expression of dignity, of respect and of justice, a solidarity which I am confident will continue to provide us with a model of social engagement that will endure."

Addressing the issue of culture cross-over, Columban, Fr. Hugh MacMahon in his book *Guest from the West* stated: "Helping to bring the good news message across cultural barriers to have it enrich other religious traditions, and in doing so have your own understandings deepened, sounds demanding, but is worth the effort."

Prof. Aloysius Lugira of Boston College, delivering a lecture on *The Catholic Church and Development in Uganda* at Georgetown University in Washington on 4 December 1999 pointed to the contribution of the Catholic Church to the development of Uganda. He said: "Since the arrival of Catholicism on the Ugandan scene development has been affected in a variety of areas that include religion, education, healthcare, economics, jurisprudence and politics. In the area of education, the Catholic Church has shouldered the leadership of establishing educational facilities at all levels, including the numerous primary and secondary schools, and tertiary institutions of education. The contribution of the Catholic Church to development in Uganda is indelibly written in the annals of Uganda for every one to know."

On 3 August 2010, Mary Robinson, as President of Realising Rights, wrote to Sr. Dr. Hilary Lyons MSHR to say: "I have just returned from a visit to Sierra Leone and felt compelled to write to you to congratulate you on your outstanding achievements over four decades in Sierra Leone. Your dear friend, Dr. Komba Kono, Minister of State in the office of Vice President, speaks very highly of the contribution you have made to improving healthcare standards in Sierra Leone and particularly in Serabu hospital."

Archbishop Julio Murat, Apostolic Nuncio to Zambia in his homily at Mass in January 2016 to celebrate the bi-centenary of the Religious Sisters of Charity recognised their preferential option for the poor. He said: "On this occasion of the bi-centenary celebration of your congregation, we can acknowledge that your motto continues to inspire you as you contribute positively to the lives of the poor people bearing in mind the signs of the times as you respond to new challenges. By your presence in Zambia and particularly in your service to the poor in the areas of education, pastoral work and health care, you have strived to actualise your love for the needy."

When Tipperary-born Fr. John Ryan SPS was appointed bishop of Mzuzu in Malawi in April 2016, Fr. Vincent Mwakhwawa, National Director of the Pontifical

Mission Societies in Malawi remarked: "Fr. John Ryan, bishop-elect of Mzuzu is another gift of faith to Malawi from Ireland. As a country, we have every reason to be grateful to God for the gift of the Irish Catholic faith. Thanks to the Irish people." That is typical of the appreciation of Irish missionaries by their host churches in the south.

Recognition of the work of missionaries also comes from the political world. Kenya's Senator Beatrice Elachi lauds the quality services provided by missionaries and the Catholic Church in her country. Speaking during a reception in the Apostolic Nunciature in Nairobi on 13 March 2015 to mark the second anniversary of the election of Pope Francis to the papacy, Senator Elachi said: "As we observe this historic day, I note with satisfaction the close and fruitful relations that happily exist between Kenya and the Holy See. As you may be aware, about 30% of the Kenyan population is Catholic. In addition, the Holy See has 26 Catholic dioceses in Kenya which are actively engaged in the social ministry through various programmes especially in the education and health sectors.

"It is also worth noting that the Catholic Church is the largest non-state provider of healthcare services in Kenya. It has an expansive network which consists of close to 500 healthcare units and over 50 community-based orphanages and vulnerable children's programs. The church works hand in hand with the government to

Local Chief, Balus K. Wakili, in Zhiko, Nigeria meeting Sr. Geraldine Henry, Daughter of Charity and board member of Trócaire during her visit to the area in 2015 *Daughters of Charity*

provide affordable services to millions of Kenyans, especially in rural areas.

"Early education in Kenya is attributed to the missionaries who not only set up schools but also ensured that quality services were provided. Currently the church has over 8,000 primary and secondary schools, five colleges, a fully fledged university, and also provides facilities for people with special needs. We applaud the exemplary work done by the Church particularly in the health and education sectors in this country. These programs and other noble initiatives have indeed gone a long way in improving the quality of life of the people of Kenya and the socio-economic development of the country."

That unique international reputation not only sheds positive light on our missionaries but it benefits the Irish state on the world stage. It is a reality that is acknowledged by the Irish state. The President of Uganda, Yoweri Museveni, paid a state visit to Ireland in October 2000. Speaking at a state dinner in his honour, the President of Ireland, Mary McAleese, emphasised the role of missionaries in relations between the two countries. "We enjoy deep, warm and cordial friendship," she said. "Among the many links between Ireland and Uganda which long predate independence and which have kept communication fresh between our two countries is the work of Irish missionaries in the fields of health and education. It is a matter of pride to us that you personally hold in particularly high regard the work of the Franciscan Missionary Sisters for Africa who educated your daughters," she concluded.

On 14 January 2016, the President of Ireland, Michael D. Higgins speaking after he received an award from the Republic of Chile at Trinity College Dublin was clear

Pope Francis listens attentively to Sr. Mary Killeen RSM in Nairobi during his visit to Kenya in 2015

Dr. Pragati Sherchan

in his view on the contribution of Irish missionaries in Chile. He said: "I recall too the extraordinary work carried out by Irish missionaries in Chile during the darkest years of the dictatorship, and I am delighted that they have also been honoured with this award. Throughout the seventeen years of military dictatorship, the Columban Fathers coordinated their efforts with the Vicariate of Solidarity which was set up by the then Cardinal Archbishop of Santiago, Raul Silva Henriquez, to offer refuge and support to victims of human rights violations. They also participated actively in the anti-torture movement, Sebastian Acevedo."

He continued: "Tragically, the Columban Fathers suffered terrorism themselves, and very directly, when their house was stormed in 1975, resulting in the murder of their housekeeper, Henriquetta Reyes, and the detention and torture of Dr. Sheila Cassidy. Two Irish Columban priests, Fr. Brendan Ford and Fr. Desmond McGillicuddy, were ultimately expelled by the junta in 1983. The actions I have mentioned of those courageous Irish priests in Chile are emblematic of the selfless work of Irish missionaries around the world as they seek to protect the dispossessed and underprivileged," he concluded.

Speaking in October 2015 as Patron of the Friends of the Missionary Sisters of the Holy Rosary about the work of the sisters, Sabina Higgins, wife of the President of Ireland, referred to "the vital role they and other missionaries have played in providing for the health, educational, and spiritual needs of people in the developing world. The sisters were known in particular for the respect they displayed towards the people they lived among and their cultures. The legacy of the sisters' work is that they developed sustainable schools, hospitals, and development projects that continue to serve the people and are staffed today by citizens of the countries where the sisters were working." Noteworthy are her references to the sisters' respect for other cultures, how they also provided for the spiritual needs of local people and how they empowered them to take responsibility for their own affairs.

In his book *To Cape Town and Back* published in 2008, the late Fr. Michael Crowley MSC recalled his conversation with Nelson Mandela on 12 July 1991 in the Cape Sun Hotel in Cape Town, South Africa. "Mandela went on to praise the church's support in the dismantling of apartheid. He mentioned Cardinal McCann, Archbishop Hurley, Archbishop Naidoo, Archbishop Henry, and Fr. Brendan Long from Scariff in Co. Clare whom he knew as the Catholic chaplain who visited Robben Island for twenty-five years, and for whom he often read the first lesson. In later years he would again meet Brendan at the conferring of an honorary Doctorate of Laws at NUI Galway. Mandela commented 'this man visited us when few others did'. He paid tribute to the many Irish religious sisters and brothers who provided education and health services, and commended the teaching sisters who were the first to accept black and white children in their schools."

There is widespread consensus in Ireland that our missionaries were at the frontline in building the unique reputation that this small country enjoys throughout the world. That reputation was emphasised by the President of Ireland, Mary McAleese when she visited the Missionaries of the Sacred Heart in Cork in May 2009 as part of the celebrations of the centenary of their arrival in Ireland. She said: "Irish missionaries are held in respect and in friendship around the world. I travel to many countries, and am always greeted as a trusted friend... not because of who I am but simply because I am Irish. The reason for that respect and friendship is the work of our missionaries in providing educational facilities for poor people, for initiating health services for them, and above all showing that they cared for strangers in foreign lands."

The same message of relationship building is clear in the statement of welcome by the Irish Ambassador to Zambia, Seamus O'Grady on his embassy's website where he says: "The relationship between Ireland and Zambia dates back to the pre-independence period of our two countries. Irish missionaries first came to Zambia in the early part of the 20th century establishing a relationship of friendship, trust and solidarity that continues to this day. In the decades that followed Zambia's independence this relationship continued to grow, and today Ireland and Zambia continue to enjoy a warm and special relationship." It is also this "relationship of friendship, trust and solidarity" that confers a very unique value on the engagement of missionaries with local communities in the Global South within which they enjoy a very "warm and special relationship."

Sinead Walsh, Ireland's Ambassador to Sierra Leone tells visitors to her embassy's website: "The formal relationship between Ireland and Sierra Leone dates back to 2005. However, Irish missionaries first came to Sierra Leone over 150 years ago, establishing a relationship of friendship and solidarity that endures to this day."

In an interview with *The Independent* newspaper in Kampala in February 2015, the Irish Ambassador to Uganda, Donal Cronin, pointed out: "The 20 years in which the Irish embassy has been here in Kampala has built on many decades of strong cooperation between our two countries going back to the 1800s when Irish missionaries first came to Uganda. The missionaries did great work in terms of establishing health clinics and education facilities. Then, right on to the 1960-70s, Irish NGOs started operating in Uganda."

African countries reciprocate the same message about friendship. For example, the website of the Kenyan embassy in Ireland states, "Kenya and Ireland have enjoyed a long history of friendship and cooperation beginning with the presence of Irish missionaries in Kenya many years ago."

I

Governments and Beneficiaries Appreciate the Work of Missionaries

The President of Kenya, Uhuru Kenyatta speaking during the *Faith for Life: Ending Preventable Maternal Deaths in Kenya Inter-Religious Consultative Forum* on 4 March 2015 described very well the appreciation and esteem in which FBOs are held in his country. These are his words: "In Kenya, about 40% of health facilities are managed by private, not-for-profit organisations which are chiefly faith-based. The role of religious leaders in maternal and new-born health provision can, therefore, not be ignored. Religious leaders are at the core of community and play an important role in shaping its opinions, values, and practices. The clergy have well-established networks, capacity to reach rural and hard-to-reach populations, and they are respected and trusted in local communities.

"Faith-based organisations have also helped to bridge the gap in healthcare through the provision of primary health care services to the people. Apart from maternal health services, they also provide immunisation, emergency relief services, and training of healthcare workers. In view of this important role that religious organisations play in the community, over and above their spiritual role, I reiterate

Br. John Conway OH accepting a Presidential Award to St. John of God Brothers on National Health Day in 1999 for their contribution to mental health services in South Korea. Looking on is Bro Thadu Kang. The congregation also set up the first alcoholic treatment centre and the first hospice in the Province of Chollanamdo   *St. John of God Brothers*

the call to action to end preventable maternal deaths in Kenya, and invite religious leaders to re-dedicate their efforts to this noble cause," he said. This president's depth of understanding of both the development and the spiritual roles of faith communities is noteworthy.

When Italian nun, Sr. Irene Stafani, was being beatified at a ceremony attended by over 100,000 people at Dedan Kimanthi University of Technology at Nyeri in Kenya on 23 May 2015, President Uhuru Kenyatta, Deputy President William Ruto, and Past President Mwai Kabiki joined the faithful in paying tribute to her contribution to Kenyan society.

President Kenyatta told the gathering that although Sr. Irene "had a better life back in Italy, she decided to forgo the comfort of her family to follow God's calling to come and serve in Africa. She had no relative here in Nyeri but came to give the word and use her talent to serve all who were around her. Her life is proof that the greatest contributors to the well-being of society are the good actions of individual members. It is not big government and everything we do, it is the single individual's life and work that can begin the process of changing communities, bring peace and healing."

The President thanked missionaries for their work, and assured that the government will continue to partner with the church in providing services to communities to improve livelihoods. Past President Kabiki told the audience: "From Sr. Irene's beliefs and values, we learn that courageous, good deeds are the gears that change the world by transforming the fortunes of humankind." These comments reflecting the importance of 'beliefs and values' illustrate the appreciation of the work of missionaries by governments in Africa.

It is, therefore, not unusual to find state health service staff working in programmes run by missionaries, especially in African countries. That is a means by which states demonstrate their practical support, and it helps community alignment with state or local government strategies and plans.

Komakech Michael Comboni, Senior Secretary, Pabo Sub-County Local Government in Northern Uganda points out: "As local administrator for local government who is responsible for overseeing the performance of all development partners operating in the sub-county, I co-opted Rev. Sr. Mary Costello, the chairperson of WACFO, to be a member of the Pabo Sub-county Technical Planning Committee to allow her to attend meetings of local government committees in which she would have opportunities to learn how the local government system operates, share success stories in her organisation by way of reporting, and benefit from technical experience and knowledgeable staff employed by the organisation." This is an example of meaningful partnership in practice.

Saint Mary's College at Vigie in Saint Lucia was managed by the Presentation

Brothers for many decades. In a speech on Presentation Day on 21 November 1976, the Governor Sir Allen Lewis said: "The advent of the Presentation Brothers in 1947 marked a turning point in the management and growth of St. Mary's College. Their breadth of vision, their concern for the welfare of the community, their administrative ability, scholarship and devotion to duty and to the welfare of their students have brought great benefits to St. Lucia. I should like to take this opportunity to express publicly the appreciation and gratitude of the people of St. Lucia for the work the Brothers have done and continue to do among us." This unique contribution by Irish missionaries was recognised by the awarding of MBEs to Br. Canice Collins in 1949, to Br. Macartan Sheehy in 1974, and to Br. De Lellis Sullivan in 2013.

In the 1970s, Sr. Rita McStay CP set up Gaborone Commercial College in Botswana. At the official opening of an extension on 17 May 1977, the British High Commissioner commented: "The school was started by the enthusiasm and dedication of priests, sisters and laymen connected with the Catholic Church, but from the beginning it was envisaged as a service for the whole community. That the school has attracted students from all sections of the Botswana community is in itself a remarkable success." This is public acknowledgement that Irish missionaries served people of all faiths and none in their work.

Zhiko is a village in the Bwari area council in Nigeria, and is inhabited by the Gbagyi people. With few amenities, the access road is often impassable during the rainy season. There is no electricity, and water is drawn from a hand operated well. Balus K. Wakili is the local chief and is very appreciative of the Daughters of Charity mission in the area comprising a mission hospital and the Hope Centre for children with special needs. "The lives of the people of Zhiko have been greatly enriched by the presence of the Daughters of Charity. The people are very grateful for them, and hope to continue to work together with them for the good of the people," he says.

Dama is the mother of two boys in Nukuru in Kenya where Sr. Patricia Speight FMSA runs the Love and Hope Centre that was funded from Ireland. She is HIV+ which stigmatised her in her community. She says: "When no-one cared, God visited me through the Love & Hope Centre Programme as my family received support in medications and food. They also made frequent visits to my home, made us feel less lonely, made us feel loved, and all this helped us look forward to another day. They made my life and that of my family bearable. I do not know what I could have done without their help." When I visited that centre in 2014 I recall clearly a little boy of about nine years of age saying how he was lost but was found and cared for by the staff of the centre. The tone in his voice communicated his heart-felt appreciation.

Mill Hill Missionary Fr. Fons Eppink, served on the board of the Pandipieri Catholic Centre at Kisumu in Kenya – an NGO formed by the local diocese and the Mill Hill Missionaries. In February 2016 Fr. Fons told readers of *St. Joseph's Advocate* – his congregation's magazine – how he met widow Amana Ndung'u one afternoon at her roadside vegetable stall in Kisumu. She had been a beneficiary of the centre's community health programme and through a micro-credit project, granted-aid by Misean Cara, she had set up a successful business as an income generator for her family. She told him: "I am so grateful for the help I have received from the support group of the Pandipieri health programme." She is just one of the 320,000 people in informal settlements that the centre serves, including 5,000 with HIV/AIDS.

Samuel Ngoke lives in Alode in Nchia-Eleme local government area in Rivers State in Nigeria. In a comment for this book he said: "Since their establishment in my village, the Daughters of Charity have made a great impact on my people through their support. They have built many houses for poor people, and they have helped many people to establish trades. They have helped in the education of many people. People are really happy with them; they have identified themselves with my people and the local church here through their service which is very visible. My people donate to help them to carry out their work."

In her book *Beyond Faith and Adventure*, published in 2006, Irene Lynch quotes Nigerian writer and banker, Dr. Virginia Anohu who was educated by the Sisters of St. Louis. "Under the Sisters of St. Louis, we received the best education that the

Sr. Roberta Ryan SSC in discussion with a Hindu woman in Hyderabad, Pakistan   *Sr. Anne Carbon SSC*

times offered. We had relentless grooming in morality, learning and discipline. Most of us grew up to cherish the values they instilled in us," said Virginia. For the same book, Elizabeth Ekechi Okaro remarked: "Most of us who were educated by the Irish sisters have not only excelled in our various fields of endeavour but have also become mothers of well educated children in leadership positions."

Julius Nyerere, the first president of the new state of Tanzania wrote in *Freedom and Development*: "Development brings freedom, provided it is the development of people. But people cannot be developed, they can only develop themselves. There is only one way in which you can cause people to undertake their own development – that is through education and leadership." That is an apt description of the holistic development approach of the Irish missionaries, and is the reason why they became so accepted and trusted by their host communities and by host governments.

Regrettably, a small number of missionaries sexually abused children in the Global South. Apart from the terrible damage done to the abused, that deplorable activity brought disgrace on those individuals who betrayed their colleagues and the missionary movement that otherwise has such a positive record. Such misbehaviour by those individuals should not take from the overall great work done by many thousands of missionaries.

Over the past decade Irish missionaries have led the way in child safeguarding and protection in the Global South through intensive training and action. Development projects funded by Misean Cara must have a child safeguarding policy in place. The implementation of this policy is checked as part of monitoring and evaluation of funded projects. That leadership has propelled the local church and civil authorities to take similar action despite previous cultural differences in some countries. That has become another example of Irish missionaries leading the way.

II

Inter-Faith Co-Operation and Dialogue

Inter-religious dialogue is an integral part of mission. Collaboration is normal practice for Irish missionaries as they strive with people of other faiths to promote the values of God's Kingdom of peace and justice.

Sr. Elizabeth Mooney SSHJM recalls a pastor from the Pentecostal Church participating in training organised by the sisters in 1995 at Ndola in Zambia on the prevention and management of HIV/AIDS. Throughout the training he frequently expressed his appreciation for the opportunities afforded to him, saying the information enabled him to educate his own congregation.

Commending the work of the sisters he said: "The communities received support and information which had changed their way of thinking on many aspects of life for the better, not only for the present but for years to come, especially around the dreaded disease of AIDS. A vision is greater than one person, and it remains with the people to inspire and motivate long after the person has left."

In the 1990s, when approached by Muslim leaders in Kamwokya in Uganda who were concerned about the spread of the HIV virus, Sr. Miriam Duggan FMSA and her Education for Life team provided training for that faith group whilst respecting their ethos. Many other congregations can point to similar inter-faith co-operation in their mission work.

Interfaith dialogue was evident at the international conference *Mission Today & Tomorrow* when journalist Amina Kazaure, Muslim Co-Ordinator of the Women's Interfaith Council in Kaduna State in Nigeria spoke and thanked the organisers for: "The rare opportunity as the only Muslim to speak at a gathering of learned Christian missionaries who have immeasurable experience in their interaction with both Christians and Muslims in many parts of the world." She told delegates: "One of the critical issues of interfaith work is to help Christians and Muslims, especially, to understand that coming together is an avenue of understanding each other so as to grow in mutual respect and be able to co-exist together meaningfully and peacefully."

Speaking about the need for tolerance, Amina said: "We must help our people to understand that difference is a natural phenomenon. We must seek to understand our cultural and religious differences and work out modalities on how we can transform them into something that can yield golden fruits and be a blessing. The fact is that even within our religious communities there is difference. In Christianity for example, you will find Catholics, Baptists, Anglicans, etc., but they are all Christians; In Islam also, we have Sunnis, Shiites, etc., and they are all Muslims. Since differences are natural and have come to stay with us, as human beings, the only option that remains is, either we seek to utilise our differences towards achieving positive ends, or we remain intolerant and be killing ourselves!"

Sr. Kathleen McGarvey OLA, speaking at the conference as then General Coordinator of the Womens' Interfaith Council which she initiated in Nigeria in 2010, emphasised the obligation of missionaries: "To promote dialogue and to do mission in a way that is consistent with respect for the people within their culture and their religions. Inter-faith and inter-cultural dialogue is not an option but a necessary part of any missionary endeavour," she said.

Speaking about the importance of dialogue to take culture and religion into account in development activities, she said: "Our definition of justice and of development can be understood only within a Christian or a western framework. Other peoples have their cultural understandings of development, and these are shaped and influenced by their religious beliefs and by their faith communities. Hence, to work in mission towards making present those values of God's kingdom, which we may speak of as indicative of development, necessarily implies respectful dialogue with people of other religions and cultures."

Continuing she said: "As we are told in the document *Dialogue and Mission*: "any sense of mission not permeated by [such] a dialogical spirit would go against the demands of true humanity and against the teachings of the gospel" (DM 29). In this context I would advise missionaries to ensure that all their development projects are done in dialogue with the people who are to be its beneficiaries and this must be done with respect for their cultural as well as their religious views."

The emphasis of these two conference speakers from the Muslim and Catholic faiths echoed the Apostolic Exhortation – *Africae Munus* – of Pope Benedict XVI who was explicit in his words: "It is important for the Church to promote dialogue as a spiritual disposition, so that believers may learn to work together, for example, in associations for justice and peace, in a spirit of trust and mutual help" (AM 88). It also reflects the words of Pope Paul VI in *Populorum Progressio*: "Development is another name for peace" (n.27).

Regrettably, history shows that not all members of faith communities have always adhered to these principles of their faiths, especially when religion is politicised. That emphasises the need for continuous and meaningful inter-faith dialogue at community and schools levels to create positive understanding that will influence attitudes and behaviour.

The 'Mission Today & Tomorrow Conference' report is filed in The National Library of Ireland (Call number 13B715), the TCD Library, the RDS Library, and the Central Catholic Library in Dublin. It is also available (2016) to read or download free as a PDF at: http://kimmagedsc. ie/news/mission-today-tomorrow-conference-report. A short video overview on the conference is available (2016) at www. youtube.com, and can be seen in the exhibition room in All Hallows College, Dublin

Sr. Kathleen McGarvey OLA and Amina Kazaure speaking at the Mission Today & Tomorrow Conference in 2013   *Zelie McGrath, Misean Cara*

Chapter Four

How Members of Irish Congregations in the South see the Past and the Future

In this chapter four missionaries – members of Irish-founded congregations – who are ministering in Brazil, Pakistan, Central and East Africa, and Peru, describe how they interpret the work of their congregations in the past and into the future. One clear message from each of them is that they, with very limited resources of their own, will continue to need outside help to continue the Irish missionary legacy. These are their reflections.

I

The Medical Missionaries of Mary in Brazil
Sr. Miranilza Nascimento dos Santos MMM

Each country in Latin America shares a common history in the cultural, political, economic and social spheres. Many people, especially the poor, lack the basic human needs and still have limited or no access to health, education, proper shelter, sanitation and food. This is the consequence of inequality and military dictatorship that originated from the early days of colonisation. "This inequality is persistent, self-perpetuating in areas where social mobility is low and it poses an obstacle to progress in human development," the UNDP said in 2010 in its first development report on Latin America and the Caribbean, entitled *Acting On the Future: Breaking the Intergenerational Cycle Of Inequality*.

History tells us that the first Irish missionaries arrived in Brazil in the early days of colonisation in the 16th century. They influenced the economy through farming, and business, they influenced the social life through investing and empowering people through education and Christian values that affected political ideologies. They were capable of feeling the peoples' pains and vulnerability, and they influenced their relatives and friends in Ireland to financially support the local missions. These threads of solidarity established between the Latin American countries, specifically Brazil, and Ireland, brought about social transformation and greater development, changing the lives of many people and forcing the politicians to make greater effort to provide for the basic needs of their own people.

It is in this context that the missionaries made a tremendous contribution to empower the people and resist the oppressive systems as well as working for integral human development. The Irish missionaries deserve our recognition as Brazilian and as Latin American people. They were brave religious men and women who were capable of reaching out to people and working with them so as to bring about social transformation. They empowered them, spoke their language, ate their food, danced in their rhythm, participated in their joys and sorrows. Some of them were so much one of us that they changed their native names to Brazilian Portuguese names to ensure that they are one of us. This expresses their solidarity in our pains, sorrows and joys.

Their legacy is being carried on by the local people who were empowered to change the oppressive situations. Like many other Brazilians, I was empowered by their testimony and commitment to the people. I met the Irish Medical Missionaries of Mary in my parish as they were facilitating a course for the leaders of the small Christian community. One of the sisters challenged me with her zeal, passion and commitment to the people. She challenged us to join hands and work together as a group for the changes we dreamt of. This made me reflect about what contribution I could make to my people and later to the world. I went to share with her about how her reflection made me to think about my life and she invited me to join the group of young women who were discerning their vocation.

A boys' carpentry class run by the Mercy Sisters in Mukuru slum in Nairobi   *Lucy Franks*

Pope Francis meeting Sr. Rodah and Sr. Tsige, Daughters of Charity from the DREAM Centre in Kenya in 2015
Cyrus Tora, courtesy of Daughters of Charity

She believed in me. This helped me to gain confidence and take further steps, leaving my familiar and comfortable zone, and embrace the challenge of being a missionary, share my life with the poor and other sisters from different cultures and continue the legacy of the Irish missionaries. Today we, the native Brazilian sisters, continue with the struggles of carrying the Biblical towel and basin to fetch water, washing the dirty feet of our brothers and sisters who are still marginalised. With no material resources of our own, this struggle, this work is only possible through the generous help of supporters in Ireland and elsewhere. We pray this support will continue.

Sr. Miranilza Nascimento dos Santos is a Medical Missionary of Mary, and ministers in Brazil. She holds a BA in Sustainable Human Development from the Catholic University of East Africa, and has ministered in Kenya, Tanzania, and Rwanda.

11

The Presentation Sisters in Pakistan
Sr. Parveen Barket PBVM

In 1895, Irish Presentation Sisters serving in Madras (Chennai) were invited to Rawalpindi to teach the Catholic children of the Irish soldiers in the British army. Later sisters gradually moved to other areas to set up schools. Currently the number of students in our schools is about 14,000. Education has always been a great need in this region. Recent statistics show that over 20% of children of school-going age are not in school. That indicates that education will continue to be a major need into the future.

From small beginnings the numbers of students increased quickly. Along with the English medium schools, the sisters also opened vernacular schools for children of the poor and needy. The fees in these were very low, and the sisters helped the families also by providing clothes, dry milk, cooking oil, meat and porridge. Sometimes the sisters had to go to the homes of the poor and bring the children to school. The weaker children were also given extra tuition in order to pass their exams.

Fr. Pat Galvin MSC lends support to mothers building a crèche in South Africa to care for their children whilst they go out to work   *Fr. James Mitchell MSC*

Parents saw the value of education and rejoiced that their children were the first generation of their families to be able to read and write and be successful in life. They began to realise that education is the only tool that can bring a huge change in society. Their way of living, nutrition, and hygiene conditions were all transformed gradually.

In the 1980s a great need was felt to make English medium schools available to the poor children also, so that they could move forward in life and be successful in the future. A great effort was made to amalgamate all vernacular schools with the English medium schools. Today, most of our schools are English medium as English is very important for job opportunities later in life.

In all our schools we have a variety of religious followers – Muslim, Christian, Hindu, Sikh and others. Religious education is provided to students according to their needs. In this way, as children are being educated together they gain a greater understanding of different religions. This applies also to parents and staff as they grow in tolerance and acceptance of one another, and interfaith dialogue is facilitated. In the current situation this is an invaluable contribution to global development in the area of peace and reconciliation.

Currently there are 30 finally professed and 13 temporary professed Pakistani Presentation Sisters in this country who are carrying on the ministries of schools, pastoral visitation, empowerment of women and nursing, as well as formation of new members for the congregation similar to what the Irish sisters did for decades.

Funding from Misean Cara has helped us to deliver essential services to meet great need and, thereby transform lives and communities. Education was, and remains, our main focus. When the local people are educated in sufficient numbers, they will lift the whole fabric of society, finding their way into varied professions, thus fulfilling the needs of their families and influencing national policies with values which promote the welfare of humanity.

My dream for the future is that the foundations which have been laid will expand and that, as the number of local sisters increases further, our work may be extended to serve the needs of other areas. But, in the current situation, this can only be achieved with the support of outside agencies, like Misean Cara, to whom we are very grateful for all the help received up to now.

To set up schools, everything has to be provided – land, which is very expensive, buildings, furniture, teaching requisites, teacher training and teachers' salaries, all of which are a huge burden on schools in poor areas. In the past, Irish and other foreign missionaries had financial support from their home countries and were able to undertake projects. This is not possible for the local sisters nowadays, except with the help of donors like Misean Cara. We hope and pray that this support and co-operation will continue in future to maintain and develop the legacy of the Irish missionaries in this part of the world, and thus contribute to global development.

Sr. Parveen Barket is a Presentation Sister. She is a teacher and served as Presentation Leader in Pakistan for ten years.

III

The St. Patrick Missionary Society in Central & East Africa
Fr. Samuel Mwathi Gichanga SPS

The Irish St. Patrick missionaries (SPS) have made significant contributions to physical structures and spiritual growth of the people of Central and East Africa. For example, in Malawi the value of their work is simply immeasurable. They have helped in building church communities that have become centres of evangelisation and of social and economic development, and form an important part of national infrastructure.

In the education sector, priests were involved in teaching, building and refurbishing schools, and paying school fees for children from poor families. The health sector

Br. Boniface Kyalo at the weather monitoring station at Baraka Agricultural College run by the Franciscan Brothers at Molo, Kenya
Lucy Franks

also benefited through the establishment of clinics and hospice (Zambia), and home based care programmes, especially during the crisis of the HIV/AIDS epidemic. People living with HIV/AIDS, many of whom were poor and bed-ridden, were kept alive by these missionaries and like-minded partners.

Many needy people have benefited from sustainable agricultural activities initiated by SPS members. Others without food sought and were given help by SPS priests. All of this engagement helped to transform the lives of people and communities. Schools, health care and spiritual centres were brought closer to people and eventually leaders emerged and are contributing to their continual development. St. Patrick's Missionaries have been involved in provision of social justice like the very significant 1992 pastoral letter – *Living our Faith* – that revolutionised Malawi as a nation and brought about multi-party government.

Foreign development aid from Ireland is still needed by missionaries in Malawi which is one of the poorest countries in the world, and her economy continues to grow on a downward slide. There will be a need to continue support to SPS priests and religious who are taking over the mantle from the Irish missionaries carrying forward their development and humanitarian tasks.

The church is encouraging its members to assume responsibility for self-sustainability, though this is proving to be a great challenge due to extreme poverty. Assistance from Ireland will continue helping missionaries to build capacity and empower poor communities. For example, there has been efforts for people in Malawi to come together to form credit unions, locally known as 'Bank Mkhonde', so that they can save money as well as get access to small loans which can change their lives. The Irish government and the Irish people have been generous to Malawi and SPS missionaries in Africa. Progress has been made, but we need continued assistance to help us to overcome the cycle of poverty which is a huge challenge.

Fr. Samuel Mwathi Gichanga SPS is District Leader – Central Africa for St. Patrick's Missionary Society. He is a native of Kenya.

IV

The Sisters of Mercy in Peru
Sr. Angelica Gonzalez RSM

The Sisters of Mercy arrived in El Porvenir and Florencia de Mora in April 1966 at the invitation of the Irish priests from the Diocese of Cork & Ross who had started the Peru Mission. At that time, there was an urgent need to meet basic needs

such as health and education. The sisters took over the medical clinics built by the
Irish mission to serve the poorest. They also supported the primary schools, and
initiated centres for weaving and sewing, a technical training centre, a free legal and
psychological aid centre, and a therapeutic and rehabilitation centre for drug and
alcohol abusers. They established over 20 care centres for school age children who
after their day in school go to these centres for their lunch and the care mother
helps them to do their homework before they go home.

In 1995 an Irish and a Peruvian sister began a mission in Mache at an altitude of
10,700 feet in La Libertad. The only religious congregation in the mountain area,
they built a mud brick convent and worked in the schools and 14 villages in the
region.

We must continue our works because, although needs change and the quality of
life has improved, there still remain huge pockets of poor and marginalised people.
They need to receive the necessary encouragement and help to get out of their
poverty. Without financial support from Ireland and other benefactors, our work
would not be possible.

I give thanks to God for the generosity of Ireland. Since the Irish mission started
in 1965 when the Irish priests arrived, they supported projects that benefit the

Holy Rosary Sisters Theresa Egwuonwu (Nigeria) and Kathleen Monaghan (Ireland) meet President and Mrs
Higgins during their state visit to Mexico in 2013   *Irish Embassy in Mexico*

poorest of El Porvenir, Florencia de Mora, Alto Trujillo, and Mache. The Irish priests left the Archdiocese of Trujillo in 2004 leaving a committed laity behind. Currently, in our community of eight, there are three Irish sisters. What will happen if we have no more Irish sisters? Will Ireland, through Misean Cara and other organisations, continue to support our work amongst the poor? I think it is necessary to establish and strengthen relationships and create more bridges, perhaps brotherhood or twinning between parishes here and in Ireland? When I visited Cork I saw collection boxes with the name Peru Mission in some churches. Was that because they have a commitment to Peru? Can we extend that bridge for the future relationship?

Sr. Angelica Gonzalez is a Sister of Mercy ministering in her home country of Peru.

The Sisters of St. Louis in Ghana, along with the congregation's Development Director, Ronan White, take a break from a 5-day training course in financial management delivered in Nsawam, Ghana by UK training company, MANGO. This was part of their up-skilling, empowerment and capacity building programme

Sr. Veronica Afful SSL

Chapter Five

Influence on Ireland's Overseas Aid Programme

In the 1960s the Irish government began to consider its obligation to underdeveloped countries. In its *Third Programme of Economic and Social Development 1969–1972* it stated: "As a nation we have particular responsibilities at our present stage of economic development. Not only have we an obligation to ensure that all members of society share in economic progress; by extension, we incur with progress an obligation towards the underdeveloped countries of the world." In 1973 the first structures for overseas aid were put in place.

Over many years various Irish government ministers and Presidents of Ireland have spoken about how Ireland's overseas aid programme was greatly influenced by the work of Irish missionaries. Addressing the annual general meeting of Misean Cara in Dublin on 27 June 2012, then Minister of State for Development and Trade, Joe Costello told delegates: "Irish missionaries were the pioneers in the area of development cooperation, predating our own official aid programme. Indeed, you led the way for much of what the Government is now doing in the area of development assistance. The influence of the missionaries is reflected in Irish Aid's focus on poverty reduction, on hunger, its commitment to avoiding any form of tied aid and its strong solidarity with those in greatest need."

In the context of a specific country, this position is illustrated in the following statement on the website of the Irish Embassy in Zambia: "Irish links with Zambia stretch back over a century. Long before an official bilateral aid programme was established and well before Zambia achieved its independence in 1964, Irish missionary societies were among the main providers of services in health and education in what was then Northern Rhodesia. Many of Zambia's leading citizens received their education at schools run by Irish missionaries, and many of Zambia's hospitals throughout much of the 20th century were in the care of Irish missionary sisters."

Then, in a foreword to the book *Sustainable Livelihood Approach: a Critique of Theory and Practice,* written by Prof. Stephen Morse and Sr. Nora McNamara, MSHR in June 2013, Brendan Rogers, then Director General of Irish Aid wrote: "Ireland has a proud history in relation to development cooperation. This history commenced with the development work pioneered by missionary orders which has been complemented and built upon by NGOs and by the Irish Government's own programme, Irish Aid."

In his book *Inside Irish Aid*, Ronan Murphy, former Director General of Irish Aid, says about the initiation of our overseas aid programme: "… Ireland had a huge advantage when it started out in that the missionary tradition had built up a real connection, especially with Africa, which resonated with the Irish public. None of the new EU member states had such strong connections. Whenever I met an African official or minister I would be a bit surprised if they did not reveal in the conversation that they had been educated by Irish priests and nuns. At the very least, when they heard I was from Ireland they would refer to the contribution our missionaries have made to educating their countrymen and women."

He credits missionaries with the extraordinary level of caring by the Irish people for the poor in developing countries. "Apart from word brought back by missionaries, there was little first-hand knowledge of Africa in Ireland in the 1950s and 1960s," he says. "The missionaries' story came to us through the plethora of newspapers and magazines about the developing world … oral testimony came from missionaries at home on leave who were allowed to speak from the altar or in schools about their work. The sheer scale of missionary activities is amazing. At the height of their work there were 6,000 in the field … the overwhelming view of those I interviewed for this book was that it is, above all, the missionaries we have to thank for the interest which Ireland takes in the developing world."

To put that 6,000 figure which relates to 1972 into perspective, the *Statistical Abstract for Ireland 1970-71* (page 265) shows that Ireland had 6,532 police in 1970, and 8,663 members in the army. In *The Missionary Factor in Irish Aid Overseas*, (page 31), published by Dominican Publications in 1980, Fr. Richard Quinn CSSp estimates that at least 60% of those 6,000 missionaries were engaged in development, and IMU research indicates that over 40% of missionaries then had university degrees whilst diplomas, for example in nursing or teaching, were not taken into account in the survey. That was extraordinary and highly skilled human capital as part of Ireland's technical assistance to the developing world before its bilateral aid programme was established in 1974.

Fr. William Jenkinson who played a
significant role in the setting up of APSO
Irish Spiritans

Murphy's comments are a reflection of the importance of missionaries to the approach to development that Ireland adopted. But how was the missionary influence exercised? Dr. Kevin O'Sullivan, lecturer in history at NUI Galway has undertaken extensive research and written about Ireland's overseas aid programme. In a number of widely researched articles, he sheds light on the influence – some of it subtle – that Irish missionaries and the then strong Christian values held by the Irish people and newly established NGOs had on the evolution of Ireland's development aid policy. There were also external factors such as the great famine in Ireland in the 1800s and pressure from the EEC [now EU] which Ireland joined in January 1973.

In his article *Biafra to Lomé: the Evolution of Irish Government Policy on Official Development Assistance, 1969–1975,* published in *Irish Studies in International Affairs, Vol. 18* (2007), the following extracts are self-explanatory: "In the 1960s Africa dominated the discourse on the developing world in Ireland. The Irish missionary movement created a vivid, albeit at times inaccurate, image of Africa in the minds of the Irish population. Missionary magazines such as *Africa, African Missionary, Catholic Missions* and *Missionary Annals* provided a window on African life. The 'Penny for a Black Baby' campaign called on Irish citizens to support missionary societies building schools, hospitals and churches in their parishes.

"A growing number of university graduates and tradesmen and women also worked in the developing world; *Catholic Missions,* for example, in July 1962 praised the emergence of a 'new class of mission lay helpers', whose efforts were important to the continuing development of links between Ireland and Africa. An increasing number of Irish people also worked with international organisations such as the United Nations Development Programme (UNDP). Their accounts informed conceptions of Africa at official levels. Frank Aiken, Minister for External Affairs from 1957 to 1969, consulted with Irish bishops working in Africa, including on ODA issues.

"Missionary orders and their publications began to view development in different terms. A November 1970 editorial in *Africa* commented that the goals of evangelism and development were, "not mutually exclusive, rather the one complements the other." In 1973 the Irish Catholic Bishops made this link explicit by founding Trócaire. Each of these commentaries served to reiterate the new position that ODA had in public debate, while simultaneously emphasising the distance left to make up at both private and official levels.

"The Inter-Departmental Committee on Development Assistance, set up as a result of the re-think of policy, met too infrequently to have any lasting impact. The reaction of the Dept. of External Affairs to proposals put to the government by a working group headed by Professor George Dawson of Trinity College Dublin

– and whose members included T.K. Whitaker, T.J. Barrington, Vincent Grogan of Africa Concern, Dr Joseph Barnes of the Tom Dooley Foundation, the Holy Ghost priest, Father William Jenkinson, and Garret Sheehan, who had served in Africa under Oxfam – provided a further example of the government's relatively conservative approach.

"The working group's September 1971 proposals aimed at the creation of a 'balanced programme of overseas aid by way of personal service' with a central Irish organisation to co-ordinate the activities of Irish volunteers, financed largely by state grants. The programme, it was envisaged, would be run by a council, on which representatives of various government departments and official agencies would sit. Reflecting the broader concerns of the post-1969 period, the proposals were the culmination of a consultation process begun by a Gorta sub-committee and adapted by others, including the Irish Missionary Union, before reaching their final form under Dawson's supervision."

After a lot of discussion and disagreement between the Dept of Finance and the Dept of Foreign Affairs, plus a change of government, the new and pro-aid Minister for Foreign Affairs Dr. Garret Fitzgerald told Dail Eireann on 9 May 1973 that he had obtained government agreement in principle for a new agency. In June of that year the government approved an Interim Agency for Personal Service in Developing Countries that became the Agency for Personal Service Overseas (APSO) in March 1974.

APSO was to provide a maximum of 75% of the cost of volunteers whom it co-financed with Irish voluntary organisations. At a meeting of the Interim Agency on 6 December 1973, the IMU offered co-operation in training and the provision of lecturers – an offer that was greatly appreciated in view of the wide experience of missionaries in developing countries. That meeting also decided to replace the term 'volunteer' with the broader concept of 'personal service' which was closer to the language of missionaries.

Records in the IMU archives show that two men – Dr. T. K. Whitaker, Governor of the Central Bank, and Fr. William Jenkinson, Executive Secretary of the IMU – were key players in the process that led to the establishment of APSO. Whitaker, as chairman of the working group, consulted extensively with Fr. Jenkinson who obviously had detailed information from missionaries about actual needs in African countries as well as volunteering models. An IMU survey had revealed "a desire for as many as 650 skilled lay volunteers." Information also came from other Catholic sources. For example, Fr. Roderic Crowley CM of the Catholic Secretariat of Nigeria in a letter to Dr. Whitaker on 8 January 1972 listed the need especially for doctors, nurses, and teachers, in particular pointing out that the Commissioner for Education had asked him for help in the provision of teachers.

Feeding stations are still common in many regions in the global south. Here children gather to be fed at a Benedictine Sisters' mission school in Lisanjala, Malawi that is funded by donors in Brazil

Courtesy World Missions Ireland

Dr. Whitaker who had written about world poverty in *Administration* in spring 1971 was very well informed, and was passionate about the needs of the developing world. He made great effort to reassure nervous Dept. of Finance officials about public funds being given to an external agency or the danger of over-dependency on public funds. In a letter to the Dept. on 10 January 1972 he stated: "The Catholic missionary bodies are spending millions and supporting thousands of people, including an increasing proportion of lay people. The realistic view is that the existing organisations are so committed that they are most unlikely to relax their efforts."

Dr. Whitaker was appointed first Chairman of APSO by the Minister for Foreign Affairs in 1973, and Fr. Jenkinson – a Spiritan missionary – was appointed one of eleven directors of the new semi-state body. Kevin O'Sullivan points out that APSO: "built on strong foundations developed through Irish missionary involvement in education and welfare provision, in the link they created in Ireland with the developing world, but also in the increasing involvement of lay Irish graduates in development work through organisations like Viatores Christi and later Concern."

Many missionaries served on the Board of APSO over the years. The latter members were Mill Hill priest, Fr. Des McGillicuddy – the IMU Justice &

Development Officer – who served from 1995 to 2000; he was succeeded by Sr. Teresa Walsh and Sr. Margaret Quinn of the Missionary Sisters of the Holy Rosary until 1st January 2004 when APSO was closed. Members of other faiths also served on the board.

But as the inter-departmental haggling continued, it was not until 26 April 1974 that the government agreed an official aid programme under pressures from its commitments to the EEC, from the discussions leading up to the Lomé Convention in 1975, and from the Irish public who were influenced by the horrible stories of missionaries about starvation in Biafra due to the war there. The new bilateral aid programme involved direct assistance from Ireland to developing countries rather than the previous contributions to international organisations to be managed by them through their own programmes.

President Mary McAleese (centre), and Minister of State Liz O'Donnell (left) visiting Sr. Miriam Duggan FMSA at the Buluba Leprosarium in Uganda in 2001   *Franciscan Missionary Sisters for Africa*

Other Events that Influenced Public Opinion and Policy

In a lengthy article – *Ireland, Africa and the End of Empire 2012* – published by Manchester University Press, Kevin O'Sullivan refers to other events in the Catholic Church that influenced public opinion and policy on overseas aid. These included: "Pope Paul VI's 1967 encyclical *Populorum Progressio* and the widespread involvement of Catholic missionaries in projects on the ground woke large sections of western society to their obligations in less well developed countries."

"The Irish Commission for Justice and Peace, formed by the Catholic hierarchy in October 1969, provided an organised voice for the church's new aspirations in international aid. The following year it published *The Third World War*, a short booklet written by its secretary, Jerome Connolly, in which he outlined the myriad problems facing the developing world."

"Trócaire borrowed heavily from contemporary Christian teaching – notably the 1971 document issued by the international Synod of Catholic Bishops, *Justice in the World* – to emphasise the pursuit of justice and human rights. Under the eyes of its director, Brian McKeown, the 'new' organisation established by the Catholic Bishops set out to offer a channel through which Irish Catholics could 'express their commitment on an ongoing basis to the needs of the Third World'. Its objectives were twofold: to distribute financial aid to various relief projects across the world, and to educate the Irish public about the issues of poverty and underdevelopment. Trócaire was immediately successful."

"Missionary activity helped to foster the kind of response seen during Concern's work to alleviate the East Pakistan/Bangladesh famine in 1971-72, but it was more frequently visible in relation to Africa, beginning with the Biafran crisis and reinforced by the continued media spotlight on disasters such as the famines in Ethiopia and the Sahel region in the early 1970s."

During that period the influence of African-based Irish Catholic bishops who pressed the Irish government to assist emerging states, it is not easy to quantify in relation to the selection of countries for aid support. Kevin O'Sullivan points out that, in this issue, it is necessary to look at the influential popular image of Africa. "The image of the continent created by missionaries in the minds of the Irish public dominated the country's perceptions of the developing world. The 'Penny for a Black Baby' campaigns and other missionary activities, including their involvement in Biafra, crudely equated Africa with poverty and under-development to a degree not associated with Asia or Latin America. Neither was the kind of extensive missionary work undertaken in sub- Saharan Africa entirely similar to that which took place in Asia.

"Although there was no strictly defined set of rules for the selection of priority states, there were several criteria common to all. Each of the states had been under British control and used English as the working language of government. The presence of Irish missionaries in each of the territories was also important, particularly as Gorta – a state development aid agency set up by the Minister for Agriculture, Charles Haughey in 1965 – had successfully cooperated with missionaries in projects in Tanzania and elsewhere."

Apart from missionaries, the influence of Trócaire's Catholic values in what we now term 'development education' within Ireland didn't go un-noticed by policy makers and the general public. Kevin O'Sullivan points out: "Announcing the results of its 1980 Lenten fund-raising campaign, Trócaire chairman, Bishop Eamon Casey told a press conference that the Catholic Church's commitment "demands of all of us an active expression which goes beyond charity and the transfer of resources and which emphasises solidarity."

But this embrace of Christian teaching was not limited to Trócaire alone. In its early years, Concern enjoyed a close relationship with the Holy Ghost missionary order, and its members sometimes described their voluntary activities as a form of new spirituality. Framing Gorta's approach in 1982, that organisation's chief executive, Ronald Smiley, reminded the public that, "If we remember we are Christian, we would recognise that it is our duty and privilege to be able to go and help those in the Third World."

The Irish state also noticed activities within the Catholic Church. Brendan Rogers in his foreword to *Sustainable Livelihood Approach: a Critique of Theory and Practice,* referred to another important landmark in the Catholic Church when he wrote: "The Second Vatican Council (1962-1965) posed a clear challenge to those working in development, such as the Missionary Sisters of the Holy Rosary, which resulted in a greater and wider engagement with rural disadvantaged communities, primarily comprising peasant farmers. This was facilitated by a number of groups initially in Ireland (particularly Gorta) that were keen to support novel ideas as a means of tackling the root causes of hunger, famine and disease – a new way of extending the hand of partnership and friendship."

Kevin O'Sullivan in *Ireland, the caring nation: foreign aid and Irish state identity in the long 1970s,* published in *Irish Historical Studies, xxxviii, No. 151* (May 2013) points out how Irish values in charity transferred into attitudes to development aid which served to put Ireland on the world stage.

"In Ireland, the translation of charity and relief into modern forms of aid began with the country's Christian missionaries, whose work in providing education and health facilities to communities in Africa, Asia and Latin America fostered a growing sense of obligation among the Irish public towards the developing world. The Biafran humanitarian crisis in the late 1960s – the first global 'famine-as-media-event', in which hundreds of Irish missionaries were involved in the provision of relief – transformed that sense of responsibility into action.

"Ireland's Christian heritage, its history, and its complex post-colonial identity all shaped domestic attitudes to the developing world, with an obvious knock-on effect on the official aid programme. The country's strong tradition of missionary activity (Catholic and Protestant) was to the forefront. Submitting their government's application for membership of the DAC (Development Aid Committee of the OECD) in 1985, Irish officials emphasised the 'long history of service in developing countries by Irish missionaries' as a significant factor in shaping its approach to foreign aid.

The progression, they argued, was obvious: "With the passage of time, these missionaries became increasingly involved in development work; and this, in turn, resulted in increasingly strong and increasingly sympathetic interest in developing countries on the part of the Irish public. There is much to be said for this assertion. From the early twentieth century, the Irish public's vision of the developing world was dominated by images from missionary magazines and the – often deeply personal – recollections of relatives, neighbours and friends who lived and worked in far-flung mission stations across Africa, Asia and Latin America. The missionary influence was equally visible in the non-governmental aid sector: the four major indigenous aid agencies (Concern, Goal, Gorta and Trócaire) collaborated with a variety of missionary organisations, while Christian Aid Ireland, a subsidiary of the British NGO of the same name, had close links with the Protestant agency, the Church Missionary Society.

"In that sense, Ireland was not significantly different from its counterparts elsewhere in the West. Quaker inspiration for Britain's early NGO culture, for example, was visible in its involvement in Oxfam. In Finland and Sweden, the work of Lutheran missionaries provided a path to countries like Ethiopia, Pakistan and South West Africa, which official aid quickly followed. The same religious influence was apparent in the NGO sector in Canada, the Netherlands and West Germany. But in Ireland, the extent to which missionary Catholicism became a specifically 'Irish' activity in the early twentieth century made aid, missionary endeavour and 'Irishness' coterminous in the minds of the Irish public to an extent not visible among its contemporaries. The missionaries' work, and that of the aid agencies that followed in their footsteps, became an extension of Irish values of Christianity, justice and peace, and their expression on the world stage.

"The churches' influence – particularly that of the Catholic Church – also extended to what Jerome Connolly described as the 'bundle of values, perceptions and inclinations' they established for the Irish state. The language and value structures borrowed from international Christian discourse provided a strong foundation for the Irish aid community, again echoing trends visible elsewhere in the West.

"The country's Christian heritage, its history of missionary activity, its strong anti-colonialism, and memories of famine generated a particularly 'Irish' attitude to aid among the Irish public. This in turn provided a strong cultural basis from which policy-makers shaped the official Irish response. The resultant policies emphasised the idealistic side of Irish state identity, finding space for history, Christian values, voluntary idealism and famine memory amid the machinations of international diplomacy."

This view was echoed by Liz O'Donnell, Minister of State for Overseas Aid in an address to the Commonwealth Business Council Conference *Action for Africa* at The Barbican, London on 5 July 2005 when she said: "Ireland's aid philosophy is central to our foreign policy; in particular its objectives of peace and justice. Our development cooperation policy and programme reflect our longstanding commitment to human rights and fairness in international relations. Our approach is also very much influenced by our history. Ireland has a long and proud tradition of active participation in missionary and humanitarian work in the world's poorest countries, which has shaped our model of aid. We have no agenda in Africa except to help. We have no colonial past, except of course that we ourselves were a colony of Britain, up until 1921." She then went on to refer to the distant memories of the famine in Ireland in the 1800s that was another influencing factor.

Kevin O'Sullivan points out: "To view aid solely as an extension of the country's Christian traditions, however, would ignore the other, equally influential, factors that shaped Irish attitudes to aid and the developing world." That is true, but it is worth noting that Ronan Murphy in *Inside Irish Aid* admits: "One official recalled looking up papal encyclicals for inspiration when making the case for funding to the Department of Finance."

SMA priest and historian, Dr. Edmund Hogan, in his book *The Irish Missionary Movement – A Historical Survey 1830-1980* (Gill & Macmillan, 1990, page 138) states: "In the post-Vatican II era the church participated in the formulation of modern development theory through papal encyclicals and exhortations like *Populorum progressio, Octogesima adveniens, Evangelii nuntiandi* and the synodal document, *Justice in the World* … Irish missionaries, it must be said, have been involved more in the application than the formulation of the Christian development model."

He goes on to say (page 139): "There can be little doubt that the church had exercised an influence on the evolution of government policy towards development.

Missionary bodies, both individually and collectively, have done much over the years to create an awareness of social and economic needs in developing countries and in highlighting justice and peace issues." He concurs that there were other influences at work which also had an impact such as the Charter of the UN in 1945, and Ireland's membership of the EEC in 1973.

What is very difficult for historians and researchers to discover are the personal relationships that existed between many missionaries and politicians and ministers here in Ireland, and with Irish diplomats in the Global South. Many in the political world have had family members, relatives, or neighbours in the religious life or who volunteered overseas. When Mrs Sabina Higgins, wife of the President of Ireland, spoke at a recognition awards ceremony in Dublin in November 2013 for Irish missionaries who had devoted over 40 years to overseas mission, she proudly mentioned members of her own and her husband's families who were missionaries. President Higgins also alluded to this family connection in his address to the annual general meeting of Misean Cara on 27 May 2015.

During the Biafran war the strength of the Irish missionary connection with Nigeria was extensive. At the beginning of the crisis there were 1,449 Irish missionaries in Nigeria with about half of them in Biafra, and several more from the Protestant faiths there too. It is easy to imagine how much contact they and their families and friends had with Irish diplomats and with politicians and ministers in Ireland. The influence of those contacts will never be quantified. Influencing the attitudes of policy-makers can be informal and very personal, but significant nonetheless.

Based on the evidence that Kevin O'Sullivan has published, plus the statements of politicians and Irish Aid officials about the influence of missionaries on Ireland's overseas aid programme, it is reasonable to conclude that that internationally recognised programme is a part of the lasting legacy of our missionaries.

Missionaries often served on Irish Aid bodies and contributed to discussion on the aid programme. In August 2002, Fr. Gerard O'Connor CSsR was appointed to the Advisory Board of Irish Aid, and in 2003 became chairman of the newly established Audit Committee of the Dept of Foreign Affairs until 2009. Fr. P.J. Gormley SMA was appointed to the Development Education Advisory Committee for a two-year term in January 2003.

When the Irish Government issued its first White Paper on foreign policy in 1996, Sr. Dr. Mona Tyndall MSHR, in a submission, advocated for aid to be an integral part of foreign policy which it subsequently became. On 1st April 2003, Sr. Dr. Hilary Lyons MSHR, as President of the *Sierra Leone–Ireland Partnership* led a delegation to meet the Oireachtas Joint Committee on Foreign Affairs seeking to have Sierra Leone included as a priority country in the Irish Aid programme.

With typical missionary values and advocacy zeal, she told the Committee: "Of all the things that have been mentioned, foremost in my mind is the rural situation. Those areas have been devastated. When the people return to their communities, they find their houses destroyed, their coffee trees and oil palms not pruned, their farms overgrown with bush. To get them rehabilitated, I would see, as a top priority, the provision of aid to the rural communities. It is not the amount of money we provide, but aid workers getting out there to deal with the situation. When the country was not safe, many of the aid agencies stayed in the large towns." In 2005, Ireland opened a diplomatic and development aid mission in Sierra Leone which became a key partner country in the Irish Aid programme in 2013.

In 2012 and 2013, missionary interest in government White Papers increased with seven well thought-out submissions from congregations to consultation papers on Irish Aid and on foreign policy – an indication of a maturing engagement in the formulation of public policy on international development.

II
One Congregation's Engagement with Structures for Development

The war in Biafra in south eastern Nigeria changed the way Ireland understood the outside world. The moving images of starving children and the 'Penny for a Black Baby' fundraising campaign by missionaries propelled stark images of suffering and death into classrooms and Irish homes. This brought about profound change with the emergence of a number of NGOs that have grown to become recognised leaders in the area of international development and humanitarian aid.

Many missionary congregations were very much part of this change, but space limits mention of only one – the Holy Ghost Fathers, now known as the Spiritans. They decided formally to actively support development activities that involved the setting up of a number of NGOs to respond to new needs and new situations in the Global South. Uniquely, the congregation's 1988 Irish chapter (meeting) expressed its support for "those confreres involved in development education, relief and refugee work." The 1994 chapter repeated this support and added: "and for those working in the areas of AIDS, ecology, women in development, and the rights of children."

We have seen earlier in this chapter the part played by Fr. William Jenkinson in APSO. One of the forms of mission that the Spiritans took on with considerable courage and enterprise was the care of the starving and displaced, particularly in

Africa. This work started with a response to starvation during the war in Biafra where many Spiritans were ministering in 1967–68, and it expanded over the years. John and Kay Kennedy, who had been Viatores Christi lay missionary volunteers in Nigeria, along with John's brother Fr. Raymond, set up Africa Concern (now Concern Worldwide) in 1968 which quickly became a major response by the Irish people to the crisis in Biafra.

An article in the *Irish Times* on 3 April 1997 on Fr. Aengus Finucane's retirement after 17 years as CEO of Concern stated: "Back in 1968, Aengus Finucane was one of those young priests in the thick of great events. In his parish at Uli, the only good road was converted into an airstrip. Up to 40 flights a night ferried in much-needed relief supplies under cover of darkness, where they were hurriedly unloaded by Finucane and his parishioners. Biafra made the world a smaller place. Here were priests – of all people – standing up to international authority and siding with the people they were ministering to. Ordinary Irish people realised, perhaps for the first time, that this country could – and should – help in emergencies in distant lands. The result was the formation in 1968 of Africa Concern, a motley collection of Catholic and Methodist missionaries, lay workers and others who came together to charter a ship to bring emergency supplies to Biafra." Fr. Aengus knew how missionaries could lead what we now call development and humanitarian aid efforts.

Fr. Aengus Finucane worked for Concern in Bangladesh, Thailand, Gabon and Uganda. His brother and fellow Spiritan, Fr. Jack, was one of Concern's field directors for many years, especially in Ethiopia. Fr. Michael Doheny was deeply involved for nearly 20 years in field-work for Concern, notably among the refugees in Bangladesh in the 1970s, as was Fr. Tony Byrne, who became a specialist in development aid and refugee situations, writing three practical guide books – *Integral Development* (1983), *Working for Justice & Peace* (1988), and *How to Evaluate* (1988), published by Mission Press in Zambia. Concern – part of the missionary legacy – now ranks amongst the leading NGOs of the world.

Prof. David Dickson, Professor of Modern History at TCD in reviewing the book *Believing in action: Concern: the first thirty years, 1968–1998* in *History Ireland* pointed out how: "The soft influence of the churches in this story is everywhere evident, symbolised by the extraordinary service of the Finucane brothers. But against this are the stories of numerous volunteers and professionals motivated by a sense of social justice that was not ostensibly religious but influenced nonetheless by the missionary legacy that had helped to create the space for Irish interventions in Africa."

Fr. Kevin Doheny, brother of Fr. Michael, who as welfare officer of the Catholic Secretariat in Addis Ababa from 1972–1980 was pivotally involved in the setting up the Consortium of Christian Relief and Development Association (CCRDA) in Ethiopia in May 1973 – the first such body of its kind in the country. He was approached by two government officials, Ato Desta Girma and Ato Kassa Kebede, and asked what the Catholic Church could do for the victims of the famine which was raging in the Provinces of Wollo and Tigre. He assured them that the Catholic Church would play its part. However, the churches had no tradition of working together. They didn't know or trust each other. It took two meetings to find agreement of 12 churches after a lot of groundwork by Fr. Kevin supported by Brian Neldner of the Lutheran World Federation. A great pioneering ecumenical initiative had begun.

As he states in his book *No Hands but Yours*, his experience in Biafra had taught him a lot about policy and tactics in fragile situations. Oxfam gave a large donation. Later, Spiritan Br. Gus O'Keeffe became administrator and built CCRDA into a highly efficient organisation, utilising 60 trucks to distribute supplies throughout the country. What started as a co-ordinating body has now evolved into a social transformation organisation with 213 member organisations and a clear strategic vision and plan.

Recognised for his organising ability, Fr. Kevin was asked for help by Leonard Cheshire in the setting up of Cheshire Homes in Africa which he did in several countries. In 1982 he set up the Overseas Disabled Association to create greater awareness of the needs of disabled people. He was a pioneer and innovator ahead of his time.

Fr. Michael Doheny had an interest in photography, and discovered the importance and power of images as a medium for bringing home to people the tragedies of the developing world. When footage taken with a small eight-millimetre movie camera was used by the *BBC* on *News at Ten*, he realised the power of television to communicate to the world. He had footage from remote areas that hadn't seen another camera, and he had a gift for writing. Having filmed extensively for Concern, he set up his own film company – Firoda Communications – and produced over 20 films on the developing world.

In 1989 with an alarming growth in the number of refugees and displaced people in developing countries, the Refugee Trust in the UK and Ireland was founded with Fr. Kevin Doheny as chairman and Fr. Norman Fitzgerald as Executive Director. Its first involvement was with Vietnamese refugee camps in Hong Kong and the Philippines. Focus then shifted to the Kurds fleeing before the ethnic cleansing of Saddam Hussein. The Bosnia Project was launched in 1991 with a generous response from the Irish people. By 1996 many trucks had been sent to Bosnia from a warehouse in Dublin containing medicine, clothes and food.

Refugee Trust opened an office in Kenya in 1992 to supervise welfare activities in four camps for Somali refugees. An office was opened in Freetown, Sierra Leone in 1993, and Fr. Noel Murphy was the first co-ordinator for a joint operation of Concern Universal (UK) and Refugee Trust which kept the refugee programmes in the dioceses of Kenema and Makeni supplied with emergency food for about 120,000 people. In 1994 it put a team of nurses and doctors into Rwanda to organise programmes for public health-care and to arrange the feeding of those returning to their homes, while providing them with tools and seeds for agriculture and to care for orphans and unaccompanied children. With a change of strategy in 2006, it changed its name to Vita.

Fr. Tom Rooney was ministering in Nigeria in 1967 when he was sent by Spiritan Bishop Donal Murray to the USA to raise funds for the building of a hospital in Makurdi. He established the World Mercy Fund. Its success was largely due to Fr. Tom's genius for making friends, including well-known personalities like Frank Sinatra and Sammy Davis Jnr. By 1999 the fund had financed seven 60-bed hospitals and twelve ancillary clinics in the Makurdi area which had a population of five million people. In response to many requests, the organisation gradually expanded to support many small community projects in Africa and South America to this day. Its motto is: "The greatest good you can do to another is not just to

Fr. Vincent Mwankhwawa is National Director of the Pontifical Mission Societies in Malawi. PMS supports the young churches in poor regions of the world, and is known in Ireland as World Missions Ireland

World Missions Ireland

share with him your riches, but to reveal to him his own." As well as the USA, it has offices in Austria, Switzerland, Germany, and Ireland to reduce dependence on one country. Several Spiritans have served on its board.

Fr. Owen Lambert was a co-founder of Self Help Africa in August 1984 in the aftermath of the famine in Ethiopia. It adopted a new approach to food and nutrition by providing seed potatoes to farmers there. That NGO and Gorta merged in 2012 to maximise an expertise in small-scale farming and growing family-farm businesses. In 2003, Fr. Owen founded A Partnership with Africa – an NGO focusing on training and capacity building, and research in Ethiopia and Tanzania, as well as development education in Ireland.

The Aidlink NGO was founded under Irish Spiritan auspices in the early 1980s. It funds small development projects in the Global South. It uses voluntary schemes to gather funds that it gives as seed money to be multiplied by government departments and other donors. The Spiritan colleges in Ireland have been regular supporters of Aidlink which is now an independent entity.

Headquartered in Stuttgart, Nächstenliebe Weltweit (NLW) was set up by Fr. Noel O'Meara in 2005, largely in response to the increasing visa-related difficulties faced by African missionaries seeking to fund-raise in Europe and the USA. A charitable company (working to become a foundation) under German law, it has an affiliate in Austria and an office in Dublin and raises funds in Germany and Austria.

NLW's purpose is to fund development work, primarily in Africa and is led by Spiritan and other Catholic missionaries, supporting women and children, as well as leading education works and responses to famine. With some 60 projects per year ranging in scale from €5,000 to €35,000 per project, NLW works primarily through local missionaries, overseen by the relevant diocese or congregation.

Kimmage Development Studies Centre (KDSC) was established in 1974 by the Spiritans initially to provide education and training to intending overseas missionaries, and from 1978 onwards to cater for the training needs of the growing development NGOs and volunteer sending agencies. From the beginning, the programme of studies welcomed participants of all backgrounds, cultures, nationalities, religious persuasions. To date it has accommodated students from over 65 countries, drawn mainly from Africa and Ireland, but increasingly also from Asia, the Caribbean and Latin America. Today, many of its graduates can be found in senior positions in development organisations in many developing countries. Irish Aid has grant-aided some of its work.

KDSC has entered into a partnership with NUI Maynooth to offer under-graduate and post-graduate programmes as well as other areas of mutual academic interest such as research projects, publications and professional development programmes.

Students can combine social science disciplines and/or languages with development studies – combinations that are unique in the Irish third level context.

Fr. Richard Quinn published pioneering articles on *Time for an Irish Peace Corps* in *The Furrow* in October 1974, *From Development to Justice* in 1979 with the IMU, and a book entitled *The Missionary Factor in Irish Aid Overseas* (with Robert Carroll) in 1980, as well many other articles on mission.

Many Spiritans served as part of the faculty at KDSC. Fr. Richard Quinn served as director of the centre for 19 years until a lay director was appointed. Fr. Richard also served as a board member of Gorta and of APSO at various stages. A number of Spiritans have also served on the board of Misean Cara.

The Spiritans set up SPIRASI in Dublin in 1999 as an asylum-seeker initiative which works with victims of torture and severe trauma using a holistic, multi-disciplinary model of care. Presently, it is the only such specialist centre in Ireland.

The extent of the contribution of this congregation, not just to supporting the poor and deprived in their missions but equally to the creation of development architecture and NGO structures, illustrates how missionaries led and influenced development in its infancy and how Christian values influenced the development sector, as Prof. Dickson pointed out.

There are other congregations with visionary members who have made, or are making, unique global contributions to specific areas of development such as Columban priest, Fr. Sean McDonagh, who is recognised around the world as an eco-theologian who works to raise awareness of the connections between justice and peace issues, environmental sustainability and faith. There are many others too numerous to mention here. Amongst them are those whose pioneering efforts and bravery brought many sacrifices, including the loss of their lives.

This group of medical students from University College Cork volunteered during summer 2016 to work in the OLA-run clinic in Mwamapalala, Tanzania. A number of medical students from NUI Galway also volunteered at the clinic   *OLA Sisters*

Chapter Six

The Role of Faith in International Development

The role and influence of faith in international development has been subject to considerable discussion and academic research over the past two decades in particular. What constitutes a faith based organisation (FBO) is blurred in reality because of the fluidity of organisational structures and the diversity in ways in which faith expresses itself.

The term 'faith-based organisation' currently acts as broad shorthand for a wide spectrum of organisations that deserve more specific treatment in the academic and development literature. This book uses a narrower definition that is confined to the main religions of the world. It is chiefly for their social, humanitarian, and development activities that are inspired by their deep faith and the guidance of their holy books that organisations are described as FBOs, mainly by the secular world. For example, a Catholic missionary congregation would not describe itself as an FBO because it is an embodiment of faith and spirituality that is self-evident.

Many FBOs have been providing services for centuries, but it is only since the 1990s that they have risen to prominence in policy, practice and increasingly, in scholarship. Much of the interest in religion has been highly secularised in that it focuses on the material and instrumental influence and relevance of religious leaders and faith perspectives. This instrumentalised or limited focus neglects the inter-relationship of personal, religious and spiritual transformation with broader processes of social transformation in developing contexts. There has been little consideration of the impact of spirituality, belief, religious experience and practice on community transformation, but that is now changing.

A deeper understanding of faith was illustrated by the UK's Minister for International Development, Ian Lewis at a White Paper consultation meeting in Lambeth Palace on 17 March 2009, when he said: "Faith is fundamental to understanding and relating to the world. It helps shape how we understand the opportunities and challenges of life – and how we respond to help those less fortunate than ourselves. Your voices are essential." This acknowledges that the sharing of one's faith creates the impetus to work for a more just and equal world where poverty of spirit and of mind is considered side by side with material poverty and the voice of the poor is genuinely heard in a holistic way.

Thomas Silberhorn, Parliamentary State Secretary, Federal Ministry for Economic Cooperation and Development in Germany told the conference on *Religion and*

Sustainable Development in Washington in July 2015: "Faith-based groups are oriented to the people, and development requires a people-centred approach. Sustainability needs a transformation of politics and mind-sets." At the same conference Alex Thier of the Bureau for Policy, Planning and Learning in USAID told delegates: "One of the things we know is that faith groups around the world are the providers, often the inspiration, the organization, indeed the capitalisation of that which is necessary to accomplish these goals."

In the growing body of literature highlighting the positive role faith and faith-inspired initiatives can play in eliciting social change, one of its central claims is the benefit of working through religious leaders and organisations that have the power to influence norms and values in communities where religion is an important dimension of culture. Another claim is that FBOs are repositories of social networks, and are seen as having a comparative advantage over their secular counterparts in that they adopt a more holistic approach as well as being more indigenous and grassroots-based.

In 2015, World Vision International (WVI) published a report entitled *Spirituality as a Conduit for Social Transformation* that was aimed at rethinking secular and religious assumptions in development practice. This was based on a broader research project with one of its aims being to generate insights regarding the significance for religion and spirituality in addressing widespread societal problems and encouraging attitudinal and behavioural change.

One of the findings from that research was: "Language is significant – organisations must be careful to use language that is contextually appropriate and sensitive to the worldviews and needs of the community in which they are working, avoiding secular development terminology which over-uses jargon and could be perceived as a western imposition, whilst at the same time being careful not to use religious language and approaches too extensively."

Another finding was that both secular and religious approaches to development can contain normative moral value judgements that sometimes cohere and sometimes conflict; organisations and practitioners need to be critically self-aware and reflective concerning the presence and impact of these embedded moral norms and the influence of moral values.

Missionary congregations in Ireland, operating under the auspices of Misean Cara, engaged in a collaborative process in 2012 to agree on the core values of the missionary approach to development, namely, respect, justice, commitment, compassion, and integrity. These gospel values and the ethos, beliefs, spirituality, and religious practice that flow from them are the foundation of the development, humanitarian, and social work of Catholic missionaries. Many missionaries would

Fr. Fintan Daly SMA has spent 53 years in Nigeria and has trained many young African priests for the Society of African Missions. Here he looks on happily as five young men are being ordained in Nigeria in 2015
Society of African Missions

hold that 'you cannot preach unless you put it into practice'.

A core principle of the ministry of Irish missionaries over many decades has been participation in the life of their adopted communities in far distant lands, and their living in solidarity with the poor and the marginalised in those communities. Participation, solidarity and subsidiarity are fundamental principles of Catholic Social Teaching.

Participation is defined by the *Compendium of the Social Doctrine of the Church* as when each 'citizen, either as an individual or in association with others, whether directly or through representation, contributes to the cultural, economic, political and social life of the civil community to which he belongs. Participation is a duty to be fulfilled consciously by all, with responsibility and with a view to the common good'. Participation and empowerment are core principles of a rights-based approach to development.

The President of Ireland, Michael D. Higgins described well the missionary approach to development during his state visit to Chile in 2012 when he said: "You do not impose a prescriptive model. Instead, you know that societal transformation needs the contribution of every citizen. Your efforts are most effective when you work within the local communities that have accepted you, listening to them and supporting them to realise their vision of a better and more just society where they can live in dignity."

Solidarity is much more than a feeling of vague compassion or shallow distress at the misfortunes of other people, whether near or far. On the contrary, it is a firm and persevering determination to commit oneself to the common good. That is to say to the good of all and of each individual, because we are all really responsible for all. The focus of development by missionaries is very much one of operating out of a paradigm of presence, rooted in a desire to engage across cultures and find locally appropriate responses to issues of poverty and injustice. They engage in community-driven development that empowers and enables people in an integrated holistic way.

Pope Francis recognised this solidarity in his letter to the bishops of Nigeria on 17 March 2015 when he wrote: "How can we fail to remember the priests, religious men and women, missionaries and catechists who, despite untold sacrifices, never abandoned their flock, but remained at their service as good and faithful heralds of the Gospel?"

Subsidiarity means that matters ought to be handled and decisions should be taken at a local level if possible, rather than by central authority. That principle was enshrined in the encyclical *Rerum Novarum* of 1891 by Pope Leo XIII. It was developed further in Pope Pius XI's encyclical *Quadragesimo Anno* in 1931 where it is described as: "a fundamental principle of social philosophy, fixed and unchangeable, that one should not withdraw from individuals and commit to the community what they can accomplish by their own enterprise and industry."

Minister of State for Development and Trade, Joe Costello told the annual general meeting of Misean Cara in 2012: "Missionaries are part of their community where they live and know the people, the community and their needs. Development intervention has to be evidence-based from the ground up rather than instigated in a top-down fashion without adequate knowledge of and consultation with the community."

These three principles are the foundations of Catholic faith-inspired development activities in the Global South, but that is not to claim that missionaries always get all ingredients right. These principles have been embraced by secular development and donor agencies, including state bodies.

Typhoon Haiyan hit the Philippines on 8 November 2013, affecting 14 million people, causing over 6,000 deaths and displacing over 4 million people. In 2015, Olivia Wilkinson of the Irish School of Ecumenics at Trinity College Dublin undertook research on *Faith and Resilience after Disaster: the Case of Typhoon Haiyan.* This was published by Misean Cara in February 2016.

Her report stated that: "Participants said that their faith is important for personal, familial, and community strength in the face of disaster. This strength allows them to be resilient. Their faith helps them to give meaning to the event, gives them a good attitude so that they can act responsibly following the disaster and encourages them to serve other people in their community. Religious involvement had also been important for participants to increase their knowledge of hazards. Material aspects, such as the chapel building, were noted as important for building social capital when used in community events. The predominant focus, however, was on resilience being more than just material and that faith helped with such personal and psychological aspects of resilience."

Following the Ebola crisis in West Africa in 2014/15, Christian Aid, CAFOD, Tearfund and Islamic Relief Worldwide undertook research to explore the relationship between humanitarianism and religion and to provide evidence, in real time, of the role of faith leaders in the Ebola response. The report – *Keeping the Faith: the role of faith leaders in the Ebola response* – recommended that faith leaders be included in health emergencies and in planning for recovery. It also identified the need to strengthen faith literacy among humanitarian staff, and the risk that the success of faith leaders in promoting behaviour change may lead to them being seen as a means to an end and used as passive actors to address social ills. Yet the changes they promoted came out of dialogue and a shared agenda which should serve as a blueprint for future emergencies.

One UN staff member in Sierra Leone speaking to researchers about local resistance to revised burial practices said: "The participation of religious leaders was a game changer" whilst a Banjo community member in Montserrado in Liberia said: "Religious leaders were the first ones to provide assistance to us."

A roundtable discussion hosted by University College Cork, Trócaire and DSA Ireland in Cork on 1st October 2015 to consider psycho-social supports during the Ebola crisis recommended: "Open dialogue with religious leaders is important to develop messages consistent with, and accepting of, the values of various groups." That is not surprising because faith is very important to more than three-quarters of the population in 17 of 19 sub-Saharan nations, according to research published by Pew Forum on *Religion and Public Life* in April 2010 which described that region as, "The most religious place on earth."

I
What Intrinsic Values does Faith bring to Development?
Sr. Miriam Duggan FMSA

"I came that you may have life and have it to the full" (John 10:10). These words from St. John's Gospel inspire missionaries in their ministry to the people they have gone to serve. It recognises with respect and dignity the total person – mind, body and spirit – and uses a holistic development approach that involves interventions that are sensitive to the multiple sources of influence on the development of the total person. These spiritual values foster a holistic approach that recognises the multi-dimensional needs of individuals and communities.

Through their experiences of working with people of diverse cultures, missionaries have been inspired to look at the root causes of many of the challenges they face and to address them rather than consider superficial solutions. For example, the focus on the education of the girl child which leads to the empowerment of women, improved parenting skills and reduced maternal and infant mortality. It has been well documented that without the education of women in a society, malpractices due to ignorance and social/cultural beliefs continue. In Africa, the woman is considered the stable force in the family and is responsible for the well-being, security and happiness of the children.

An important part of development is character formation of the person. Without that no amount of investment in projects will succeed fully. The intrinsic values practised by missionaries in development projects are key to the achievement of positive results. Faith values bring the added components of respect, justice, commitment, compassion, and integrity to integrated human development. Pope Paul VI in *Populorum Progressio* in 1967 pointed out: "For development to be authentic it must be complete, taking into account all the dimensions of the person and not be limited to satisfying basic material needs, but the most profound aspirations of the person and all people."

Especially when working on the margins of society, it is important to work on values that influence life-styles, and to motivate people to break with negative behaviours and to work at becoming good citizens and community members. Missionaries believe in people, motivate, encourage, and inspire them to become the people they are meant to be and that they have the capacity to succeed and "have

Sr. Miriam Duggan FMSA after receiving a Presidential Distinguished Service Award from President Higgins in 2015
Lensmen Photography and Video

life to the full" with dignity, despite disadvantages. Local communities need to see themselves as agents of their own change with the ability to exercise some creative freedom in their conditions of living through authentic grassroots participation. This is an exercise in human dignity that is foundational to Catholic Social Teaching and the work of missionaries.

In their partnership agreements with FBOs, UNAIDS, UNICEF, and UNHCR recognise the critical importance that faith values bring to humanitarian and development programmes. They also recognise correctly that these values should not be compromised in partnership initiatives.

In a message for the World Interfaith Harmony Week in February 2015, UN Secretary General, Ban Ki-moon said: "Religious leaders and communities have immense influence. They can be powerful forces for cooperation, learning, healing and – as you highlight today – sustainable development. They can set an example of dialogue, and unite people based on precepts common to all creeds. And they can point the way toward addressing underlying causes of disharmony, including poverty, discrimination, resource scarcity and poor governance."

Overcoming poverty has been a major topic in many development goals. In order to put an end to the chronic cycle of poverty, people need to value their self-worth, be uplifted and empowered through education and vocational training so that they can get employment and have the dignity of being able to support their families. This also involves knowing labour laws and their rights so that advantage is not taken of them.

In many areas the Catholic Church, through its justice commissions and missionaries with their deep motivation, has promoted these rights and advocated locally and at UN level on behalf of people especially those in poorer communities by being a voice for the less fortunate in society. Training programmes on justice issues inspire and support the educated local people to be a voice for their own people when they hold positions of authority in the future. I have witnessed this happening.

Missionaries integrate faith values in a culturally and socially appropriate manner into their development and humanitarian work which brings an added enrichment, commitment and sustainability. Building on a sense of a God presence which is deeply rooted in many African cultures in particular, the values of integrity, sharing, care of neighbour and family all help the advancement and sustainability of community development initiatives.

Missionaries bring a unique value in that they are usually there for the long haul, becoming integrated with the life of the people they serve, and they are trusted. It has also been recognised that when war and disruption erupt, they stay with the people when they most need, not only material support, but also psychosocial and spiritual comfort. I had that personal experience running a hospital during the rebellion in Uganda. They remain in solidarity with the people in their time of suffering. This solidarity has endeared many missionaries to the local people. By witnessing to Gospel values of peace, forgiveness, respect for all peoples, solidarity, and the value of the gift of life in all its forms, missionaries endeavour to bring about the Kingdom of God.

Sr. Dr. Miriam Duggan is a Franciscan Missionary Sister for Africa. Currently based in Kenya, she ministered in Uganda for over 30 years where she played a leading role in the fight against HIV/AIDS. She is the recipient of many international awards for her work including from the Parliament of Uganda and the President of Ireland.

II
There has to be a Positive Interface between Faith and Development
Dr. Duncan Green

I have worked in and with many faith-based organisations over the years and have long argued that development organisations can't afford to be blind to the importance of faith. Research by the World Bank and others consistently shows that people living in poverty trust their churches more than any other institution, and faiths are vital in forging the attitudes and beliefs that underpin the daily life of society. Moreover, the world is becoming more, not less, religious – secular Europe (at least at elite level) is the one region that is out of step. Hence, I believe there is a need to increase 'religious literacy' in the development sector, even in secular organisations.

When we think harder about how change happens, religion keeps cropping up, whether it's promoting agency and a sense of 'power within', for example, in our work on violence against women, trying to find out how poor people experience poverty, or exploring the internal structures of social movements like the Arab Spring. In all of these, religion plays a crucial part in forming identity and values.

In resilience to shocks, whether it's the global financial crisis of the past decade, or the first few chaotic hours and days after the Haitian earthquake in January 2010, poor people turn to their churches and mosques for help in an emergency. If we are serious about promoting disaster risk reduction before catastrophe hits, we need to be talking to the institutions that are most relevant to poor people.

Campaigners are trying to understand better the deep frames that determine how we see the world. Faith plays a vital role in creating those basic frames and values.

Hence, there has to be a positive interface between faith and development."

Dr. Duncan Green is Senior Strategic Adviser with Oxfam UK, and author of From Poverty to Power and several other books. He has held senior policy positions with CAFOD and the Dept of International Development in the UK. An honorary Professor of International Development at Cardiff University and a visiting fellow at the Institute of Development Studies, he writes the popular blog http://www.oxfamblogs.org/fp2p/

III

The World Health Organisation and the Faith Interface

A report – *Appreciating assets: mapping, understanding, translating and engaging religious health assets in Zambia and Lesotho* – published by the World Health Organisation (WHO) in Washington on 7 February 2007 estimated that between 30% and 70% of the health infrastructure in Africa was owned by FBOs.

The researchers argued that health, religion and cultural norms and values define the health-seeking strategies of many Africans. The failure of health policy makers to understand the overarching influence of religion – and the important role of FBOs in HIV treatment and care – could seriously undermine efforts to scale up health services.

"Faith-based organisations are a vital part of civil society," said Dr. Kevin De Cock, Director of WHO's Department of HIV/AIDS. "Since they provide a substantial portion of care in developing countries, often reaching vulnerable populations living under adverse conditions, FBOs must be recognised as essential contributors towards universal access efforts."

Ted Karpf, Partnerships Officer in the same department pointed out: "Donors and health-care funders need to take the role of FBOs into account. Without the FBOs, the hope of universal access to prevention, treatment and care is lost."

In some areas, faith-based hospitals or clinics are the only health-care facilities that exist. FBOs are also a major source of funding for AIDS particularly in some of the least developed countries, due to their capacity to fundraise from faith networks in developed countries. For example, missionary congregations in Ireland fundraise millions of Euro annually from the Irish public, apart from the state funding they receive through Misean Cara and other funding agencies.

The above report and further mapping was followed in December 2009 by a partnership agreement between FBOs and UNAIDS as part of its strategic framework. This committed UNAIDS to "refraining from attempting to discredit or undermine religious belief," and committed FBOs to "providing services based on evidence-informed practices consistent with the FBOs own faith and values."

IV
The World Bank and the Faith Interface

Better understanding and harnessing the role of faith in development is becoming an area of growing interest and engagement within the World Bank Group which along with FBOs shares the common goal of fighting poverty. For this purpose, the bank and over thirty religious leaders representing Bahai, Buddhist, Christian, Hindu, Jewish, Muslim, and Sikh organisations met in February 2014 and formally expressed support for ending extreme poverty by 2030 in a statement entitled *Ending Extreme Poverty: A Moral and Spiritual Imperative.*

Describing that statement as an 'inspirational document,' World Bank Group President, Jim Yong Kim welcomed it as an important step in achieving the poverty goal set by the World Bank Group in 2013. "The moral imperative can help drive the movement to end poverty by 2030 by inspiring large communities to act now and to advocate for governments to do the same. These commitments from religious

From left: Sr. Veronica Rop (Kenya), Sr. Wilhelmina Uhai (Tanzania), laywoman Margaret Ssebunya (Uganda), Sr. Anne Oyier (Kenya) and Sr. Marie-Rose Ndimbo (Democratic Republic of Congo) take a break during a gathering of African theologians in Nairobi focused on ethical issues and convened by Catholic Theological Ethics in the World Church   *Joshua McElwee/National Catholic Reporter*

leaders come at just the right time – their actions can help hundreds of millions of people lift themselves out of poverty. I believe that some of the most important leaders in the movement to end extreme poverty will be people of faith, people who are motivated fundamentally to help the most vulnerable among us," he said.

As we have seen earlier with UN bodies, there was good reason why the bank reached out and brought leaders of FBOs together to draft the moral imperative statement. According to a 2012 Pew research study, globally, more than 8 in 10 people identify with a religious group, and religion plays a role in forming the values, ethics, and world view of the majority of people across the world.

This faith initiative by the bank is aimed at developing the partnership with religious leaders and organisations and strengthening constructive dialogue, collaboration, and evidence around the role and contribution of faith-inspired organisations in development. "If we ignore religious communities and organisations, we do so at our own peril because these could be potential champions and allies for what the bank is doing, particularly given the amount of common ground there is with many faith traditions who also care deeply about poverty," said Adam Russell Taylor, who leads the faith initiative at the bank. He noted that FBOs play a huge role in providing vital services, such as health, education, social protection, and, increasingly, peace-building.

Sr. Annah Nyadombo (Zimbabwe), left, talking to Sr. Veronica Rop (Kenya), right, during a session at a gathering of theologians in Nairobi. In the background is Sr. Solange Ngah from Cameroon   *Fr. Lucas Chan*

Discussions between the bank and FBOs revealed how faith-inspired organisations and leaders have specific skills and assets that are critical in tackling development challenges. It acknowledged that faith leaders have a gift for delivering simple, poignant messages, and that they have the power to enact positive behaviour change. Jim Yong Kim spoke about the inextricable linkages between poverty and conflict, and the incredible potential of faith leaders and FBOs to be positive influencers in their communities, helping people choose to reject extremism and violence.

The Moral Imperative Statement is clear. It states: "We in the faith community embrace this moral imperative because we share the belief that the moral test of our society is how the weakest and most vulnerable are faring. Our sacred texts also call us to combat injustice and uplift the poorest in our midst. No one, regardless of sex, age, race, or belief, should be denied experiencing the fullness of life.

"In too many parts of the world, women and girls are consigned to second class status, denied access to education and employment, and victimised by violence, trafficking and rape. Until each and every person is afforded the same basic rights, none of us can truly flourish.

"We must also state unequivocally that ending extreme poverty without mitigating climate change and combating inequality will be impossible. Climate change is already disproportionately hurting people living in poverty. Extreme inequality, within and between countries, contradicts our shared religious values, exacerbates social and political divisions, and will impede progress. What is needed is a new paradigm of socially inclusive and environmentally sustainable economic growth.

"Our shared convictions call us to empower and uplift those living in poverty, so that they can become agents of their own transformation. Our approach to this staggering need must be holistic, rooted in the spiritual visions of our respective faiths, and built on a shared recognition of the intrinsic dignity and value of every life on earth."

V

The Beliefs and Values Missionaries Planted have become Precious Assets in Taiwan

The Government of Taiwan upholds freedom of religion but goes much further by each year recognising the contribution of foreign nationals, including missionaries, to that country. During an awards ceremony on 10 July 2007 the then Minister of the Interior, Lee Yi-yang, commended the unselfish dedication shown by 80 missionaries to his country.

Referring to their work during the 2004 tsunami he said: "These religious workers never left their stations and used their strength to significantly help stabilise Taiwanese society… In them, we see the incarnation of Mother Teresa and also the love of Christ… A total of 80 missionaries have stayed in Taiwan for an average of 37 years and 13 of them have preached in Taiwan for more than half a century. Most of them view Taiwan as their second home. The beliefs and values that they planted in every corner of Taiwan have become precious assets for us."

The President, Ma Ying-jeou at the awards ceremony in Taipei on 6 December 2011 commended the work of Christian missionaries in Taiwan saying, "Thanks to their selfless contributions there are more and more good people and good deeds being done." At the 2015 ceremony with 35 missionaries on 25 August, the then Minister for the Interior, Chen Wei-Zen remarked, "These missionaries are more Taiwanese than me." This demonstrates the value that many governments place on the contribution of foreign missionaries to their countries and how the Christian faith is respected and valued.

VI

"Faith Makes such an Important Contribution to Development," says the British Government

In 2012 the British Government launched its *Faith Partnership Principles*. In the Foreword, the then Secretary of State for International Development, Andrew Mitchell alluded to the importance of faith in development when he wrote: "Faith makes such an important contribution to development. Most people in developing countries engage in some form of spiritual practice and believe that their faith plays an important role in their lives. Faith groups can inspire confidence and trust. They are often seen as a true part of the local community and more committed to it than perhaps other groups. Indeed, they are often the first group to which the poor turn in times of need and crisis and to which they give in times of plenty. I have seen for myself in some of the most deprived and difficult parts of the world, the extraordinary work by faith groups who bring light and hope to the desperate.

"Faith groups are doing excellent work in providing not only humanitarian relief, but delivering health, education and other services in some of the most troubled parts of the world. They are making a real difference to countless lives. The work of governments alone will never be enough. For lasting change, states must fully engage with a range of civil society organisations. I recognise the unique contribution of faith groups in both delivering development and connecting with communities in the UK and abroad, particularly those that are marginalised or can't be reached by other means."

The British Government is clear on the importance of Catholic Church networks as revealed in a despatch on 22 March 2013 by the Foreign and Commonwealth Office and its Embassy to the Holy See which said: "The Holy See has a network of churches and affiliated organisations throughout the developing world, and also has links to other church organisations. Catholic networks remain key players in many parts of the world ... we have built strong relations with some of the Catholic non-government organisations ... Pope Francis' agenda in favour of the poor and the most vulnerable has provided a strong backdrop to our work to prevent extreme poverty and to protect the planet."

Prominent British atheist and former Labour Party Deputy Leader, Roy Hattersley, writing in *The Guardian* on 12 September 2005, during Hurricane Katrina in the USA, pointed out that almost all of the charitable groups involved in the disaster relief were religious. "Notable by their absence" he said "are teams from rationalist societies, free thinkers' clubs, and atheists' associations – the sort of people who not only scoff at religion's intellectual absurdity but also regard it as a positive force for evil."

VII

The Expanding Influence of Faith in Development

Faith inspired values are not exclusive to ordained or vowed religious. They also extend to many individuals engaged in development and humanitarian activities. Adi Roche, founder and CEO of Chernobyl Childrens' Project International in an interview with *The Irish Catholic* on 12 May 2009 said: "I have a very faith-based approach to work. Faith is core to both my work and life which are very hard to differentiate between." This reality is now more fully recognised within the development sector internationally.

However, some consultants and evaluators of development programmes who operate through a purely secular lens still appear to have difficulty in fully understanding or measuring the specific and intrinsic values that faith injects into such programmes and how these should be measured apart from logframes designed chiefly for northern financial accountability standards. Donors and the wider development community have drawn from all sorts of models, including from business, to focus on strategy and planning that has tended to over-emphasise the visible and tangible and under-emphasise the qualitative or very important consequences that can take place in the life of an individual or a community due to a faith-inspired development intervention.

There is often a focus on quantitative results, but qualitative outputs and outcomes are equally important as service users perceive services as person-centred. Variables in the quality of life include not just income per capita and infrastructure, but equally healthy life expectancy, social supports, well-being, happiness, the freedom to make life choices, trust, plus the aesthetic and emotional dimensions. These are indicators that need to be measured too to capture the faith-inspired holistic approach to development and solidarity for the common good of all.

Measuring performance against pre-set targets and 'what' works only, whilst not giving sufficient attention to programme contributions and contextual factors that influence results does not employ a full systematic approach – one that asks 'why' and 'how' something works – to enable understanding that may lead to transformational or systemic change.

The statement of the African Faith Leaders after meeting in Kampala, Uganda on 2 July 2014 to discuss the post–2015 development agenda said: "The focus on purely statistical approaches to measure and express human wellbeing is inappropriate and incapable of inspiring substantively qualitative changes needed to better the lives of individuals and communities."

Delegates gathered at the UN in April 2015 for the 14th session of the Permanent Forum on Indigenous Issues called for a more holistic evaluation of development, that is, measurements that include qualitative as well as quantitative, and the inclusion of indicators related to work life, social networks, environment and ecology, personal security, plus cultural and spiritual well-being in determining development effectiveness. These are important indicators that apply to faith-inspired integral human development, and each has its own value that must be taken into account. It is noteworthy that the *2016 World Happiness Report*, for the first time, gives a special role to the measurement and consequences of inequality in the distribution of well-being among countries and regions.

Today, most northern donors accept the concept advanced by Sr. Mary T. Barron OLA in the IMU newsletter in March 2007 when she said: "For the success of development, practitioners and donors must develop an understanding of cultures and their underlying spirituality and religious traditions. They must go beyond the dualistic approach which demands the separation of spirit from matter, culture from economics, and in the case of the missionaries separating the 'development work' of missionaries from the 'pastoral work' of missionaries … Whereas many traditional development institutions tend to separate materials from spiritual well-being, faith communities take a much broader view and see the causes and solution to poverty as encompassing both."

Of course, missionaries and FBOs have a responsibility to develop a theory of change that links the faith element in development to impact and effectiveness for communities so that the evidence of it can be identified and measured, as well as the value for money of their holistic approach.

In an evolving development sector, faith-inspired development agencies unite and collaborate to maximise their effectiveness. ACT Alliance, formed in 1990, comprises 14 member Christian organisations across Europe, to promote justice and peace and the eradication of poverty by influencing EU decision-making processes as they affect the Global South. CIDSE – comprised of 17 Catholic member organisations from Europe and North America – challenges governments, business, churches, and international bodies to adopt policies and strategies that promote human rights, social justice, and sustainable development. Its priority issues are development finance, food, climate justice, and business and human rights. ACT Alliance and CIDSE collaborate on some policy and advocacy issues for even greater impact.

In 2000 and 2001 Christian Aid convened a series of meetings in Dublin out of which developed the Dóchas Rights-Based Approaches to Development Working Group. The Group's aim was to promote the notion of poverty as a human rights issue through research on the concept and application of a rights-based approach to development. That approach is now common within Irish NGOs.

Fr. Seamus Kelly MSC broadcasts religious services by radio to reach a wide audience in Venezuela

Fr. Michael O'Connell MSC

Founded in 1954, Caritas International is another collaboration. Comprised of 162 relief, development and social service agencies in over 200 countries, including Trócaire, it is the largest confederation of Catholic agencies. Caritas delegations regularly represent the one million voices of the confederation at important high level international meetings and events. These include the UN General Assembly, the UN's Framework Convention on Climate Change, the G8, the World Economic Forum, the World Social Forum, the Global Forum on Migration and Development, and the Global Committee on Food Security. This illustrates the global recognition of the vital role of faith-inspired organisations in advocating for the poor and the marginalised everywhere.

The Dutch Ministry of Foreign Affairs has made great strides towards incorporating an understanding of religious contexts into its development work. The inception of the *Knowledge Forum on Religion and Development Policy* was announced in a September 2005 press release which stated: "The importance of religion and religious leaders in fighting poverty and in conflict resolution is underestimated." The Dutch Advisory Council on International Affairs published a report in 2005 on religion's influence on development. The report found: "Experience has shown how important it is for development interventions and policy to be compatible with the complex and flexible belief systems of people in developing countries. It is only by taking account of the cultures and religions of all participants that the motivation and energy necessary for sustainable development can be mobilised."

A globally significant initiative occurred in Germany in February 2016 with the launch of a new strategy on *Religious Communities as Partners for Development Cooperation* by the Federal Ministry for Economic Cooperation and Development (BMZ). Minister Gerd Müller commented: "Without the involvement of the world's religions, we will not be able to meet the challenges the world is facing. A values-based development policy takes the contribution of religion seriously. Wherever we can achieve more by working together, we will increase our cooperation with religious actors. We have laid down clear criteria in our strategy to guide us in this endeavour," said Minister. Müller.

And the German development agency is prepared to learn from this engagement. The strategy states: "We want to increase the effectiveness and sustainability cooperation by giving more attention to the religious and cultural context, and engaging with religious actors early on. To that end, we will enter into dialogue on the impacts of our programmes. Where necessary, we will further evolve our understanding of development." In line with the policy of international bodies outlined earlier in this chapter, BMZ states: "We respect our partners' spirituality, and accept that they cannot just check their spirituality in at the cloakroom before the beginning of talks about cooperation." BMZ gives €200 million in funding annually to the two umbrella development agencies of the Protestant and Catholic faiths for their projects.

Alongside this insightful strategy, Germany, with support from governments in the UK, Sweden, the USA, the UN, and the World Bank, has set up the International Partnership on Religion and Sustainable Development (PaRD) to develop common ideas on how to improve cooperation with faith communities.

In addition to the direct work of FBOs and missionary organisations, we will see in Chapter 7 the hugely important work these groups undertake at the United Nations by representing the voices of the poor and advocating for human rights and social justice from a faith-inspired holistic perspective.

Governments in the global south welcome faith-inspired development. The President of Malawi, Professor Peter Mutharika speaking at the episcopal ordination of an Irish-born missionary on 27 August 2016 said: "Bishop Ryan has been with us for a long time. As a Kiltegan of the St Patrick's Missionary Society, we have seen his commitment to education. We have seen his commitment to evangelisation and his determined passion for the youth. His teaching in the seminary and in the university; and his calling to become bishop shows us a humble servant who is committed to enlighten the minds and hearts of the world."

President Mutharika described the consecration of Bishop Ryan as a priceless gift not only to Catholics but to all Malawians. He urged the church to help change people's mindset and instil in them the spirit of patriotism, of hard work, and integrity for the development of the country. "We have comfort in knowing that Bishop Ryan has so much to offer to the church and this nation. May the Lord grant him the wisdom to make the right decisions, the courage to do what is right, and the faith to follow that wisdom," he concluded.

Chapter Seven

Advocacy by Religious at the United Nations

The UN has developed a very constructive interface with faith leaders. Its Secretary General, Ban Ki-moon has spoken publicly many times to highlight the important role of faith in world affairs.

In a message for Interfaith Harmony Week on 1 February 2013 he said: "For billions of people around the world, faith is an essential foundation of life. It provides strength in times of difficulty and an important sense of community. The vast majority of people of faith live in harmony with their neighbours, whatever their creed, but each religion also harbours a strident minority prepared to assert fundamentalist doctrines through bigotry and extreme violence.

"These acts are an affront to the heritage and teachings of all major religions. They also contravene the Universal Declaration of Human Rights, which affirms the right of all to freedom of thought, conscience and religion. It is imperative that the moderate majority is empowered to stand firm against the forces of extremism. But, this can only be achieved through strong leadership."

On 10 June 2015, Ban. Ki-moon addressed the *Congress of Leaders of World and Traditional Religions* on the topic of *Promoting Dialogue for Peace and Prosperity in Turbulent Times in Kazakhstan*. He pointed out: "Religious leaders – traditional and non-traditional – have a pivotal role to play. In times of turmoil, religious leaders can provide a values-based glue to hold communities together and provide common ground for peace-making and problem solving. You can do so by fostering dialogue; by using spiritual authority to encourage individuals to act humanely; and by promoting shared values as enshrined in the Universal Declaration on Human Rights and the International Covenant on Civil and Political Rights, and as reflected in the teachings of all world religions."

In his message to the *World Conference on Dialogue* on 16 July 2008 in Spain, he said: "There have been few periods in history when the need for dialogue among world religions has been greater. At a time of increasing divisions along cultural and confessional lines, faith communities have a crucial role to play in fostering mutual understanding and in promoting consensus on common values and aspirations.

"It is important to note that many conflicts that appear to be rooted in religion often have their origins beyond the confines of faith. Indeed, political rivalries, territorial ambitions or competition for natural resources are fertile grounds for the emergence of violence. This unique gathering of religious leaders can help debunk the dangerous myth that religion, even when properly understood, inspires violence.

"The role of religious leaders as peace builders must be reinforced. From Indonesia to Sierra Leone, from Nigeria to El Salvador, from Kosovo to Sudan, religious leaders have played, and continue to play, a prominent role in helping to initiate dialogue between warring parties, in providing emotional and spiritual support to communities affected by conflict, and in facilitating the process of reconciliation.

"We should do more to create platforms for engagement with religious leaders at the international level. For a number of years now, the United Nations has been strengthening and broadening its interaction with faith-based organisations. The Alliance of Civilisations, along with the UN Population Fund, UNESCO and other UN bodies, have been playing an important part in this process, including the advancement of new partnership initiatives and talking frankly about cross-cultural concerns."

At the General Assembly on 22 April 2015 the Secretary General urged faith leaders gathered to stand up for the collective good and amplify their voices in support of moderation and mutual understanding, warning that he fears an 'empathy gap' is causing people to turn their eyes from injustice and numbing them to atrocities.

International religious representatives at the UN attending a UN Dept of Public Information conference on Education for Global Citizenship in Seoul, South Korea in 2015. Left to right: Sr. Teresa Kotturan SCN, Fr. Guillermo Campuzano CM, Sr. Catherine Prendergast DC, Sr. Margaret O'Dwyer DC and Sr. Monique Javauhey DC   *Courtesy Sr. Catherine Prendergast DC*

"At a time when we are seeing so much division and hatred, I wanted to bring people together under the banner of the United Nations to explore how best to respond," he said at a gathering of leaders representing diverse faiths, including Islam, Judaism, Christianity, as well as ministers, academics and spiritual teachers.

"Religion does not cause violence, people do. The dignity and worth of the human person, the equal rights of men and women, tolerance and living together in harmony…these principles are our bedrock and they are what this organization defends. Faith leaders gathered today have a vast audience, great influence and an immense responsibility. We need you to promote dialogue as an antidote to intolerance. Your voices will be critical in countering hate speech and finding common ground."

At the same meeting, the President of the General Assembly, Sam Kutesa told delegates: "Religious leaders have an important role to play, and we should support them in spreading their messages of peace, harmony and hope." He urged that steps be taken to fully engage religious leaders, including greater collaboration with

The 2016 Board of UNANIMA   *UNANIMA*

the UN, with a focus on maximizing respective strengths.

Other Organs of the UN take a Similar Line

UNICEF: In the foreword to *Partnering with Religious Communities for Children,* published by UNICEF in January 2012, Anthony Lake, Executive Director wrote: "Long before there was a UNICEF, faith communities were among the greatest advocates for the world's neediest children, providing guidance, aid and comfort to millions of disadvantaged families. In fact, the Convention on the Rights of the Child – the most widely accept human rights treaty in the world – reflects deeply held values embedded within religious traditions that uphold the inherent dignity of every child and the centrality of the family in building strong communities.

"Today, faith communities continue to be an indispensable partner in UNICEF's work to advance children's rights and enhance their well-being. Such partnerships are especially important in our renewed focus on reaching the poorest, most vulnerable and hardest to reach children and families."

Apart from the benefit of the networks of FBOs, UNICEF emphasises the shared values and the moral influence and leadership that FBOs bring to activities. It states: "The Convention on the Rights of the Child expresses a holistic vision of the child that is informed by, and reflects values shared with, the world's major religious traditions, such as a holistic notion of the child and a comprehensive understanding of his or her physical, emotional, social, and spiritual needs … and the importance given to the family as the best place for bringing up a child."

"Religious communities have developed structures and defined relationships shaped by these values," it states, "and their mandates and belief systems encourage efforts to speak out on behalf of and assist the disadvantaged, marginalised, and vulnerable. Their traditions of intergenerational sharing of knowledge and faith help to sustain and perpetuate these systems."

In relation to moral influence and leadership, UNICEF declares: "Due to their moral influence, religious leaders can influence thinking, foster dialogue, and set priorities for members of their communities. For example, 74% of people in Africa identify religious leaders as the group they trust most. Religious leaders shape social values and promote responsible behaviours that respect the dignity and sanctity of all life. Many religious leaders are skilled and influential communicators who can reach the hearts and minds of millions of people in ways that humanitarian actors cannot. Because they have more access to the family and personal spheres than most outside actors, religious leaders serve as an important conduit of communication for social change and transformation. Religious leaders provide spiritual support and stability which can help meet people's psychosocial needs in the face of adversity."

UNHCR. In June 2011, the UNHCR – NGO Annual Consultations in Geneva held a special session on faith and protection. This identified many of the strengths and challenges of working with FBOs. The Official Rapporteur's Report stated: "NGOs recognise the importance that faith plays in the lives of conflict and disaster-affected communities, and the role and influence of faith communities and faith-based organizations in protection. Faith runs deep in the veins of conflict and disaster-affected communities and plays a major role in their lives. It helps people cope with trauma; it validates their humanity; it informs their decisions; and it offers guidance, compassion, consolation and hope in their darkest hours. At-risk or affected communities turn to FBOs for physical protection, material assistance, guidance and counselling, spiritual confirmation, compassion and understanding."

The special session also acknowledged that: "Many FBOs have strong links within their communities and consequently enjoy great levels of access, trust and local knowledge, which can assist delivery in complex and insecure environments; local FBO actors, from within affected communities and beyond, are often well placed to advocate for humanitarian access and protection, and to promote peace building and community-based durable solutions, and the spiritual values of FBOs can foster a holistic approach that recognises the multi-dimensional needs of individuals and communities."

This was followed by the High Commissioner's *Dialogue on Protection Challenges* in December 2012 with the theme *Faith and Protection*. In his opening remarks to the

Sr. Jean Quinn, Irish Sister of Divine Wisdom is Director of UNANIMA International. She was the founder of the Sophia Housing Association in Ireland in 1999, and served as provincial of her congregation in the UK and Ireland
UNANIMA

meeting António Guterres, the UN High Commissioner for Refugees said: "We have been working for decades with faith-based humanitarian organisations, some of which are much older than UNHCR. Local religious communities and faith leaders also play a central role in most humanitarian crises where we operate.

"Nonetheless, UNHCR has for many years tended to view these partners with the same lens as the secular-based organisations it works with. This approach, while rooted in the requirement for the organisation to act neutrally in accordance with humanitarian principles, has sometimes prevented us from considering the full potential of these organisations in helping us to address protection challenges in ways that complement our own secular approach. For one, they are better placed to address the spiritual needs of communities affected by conflict, disaster and displacement. Even more importantly, in most circumstances local religious communities are the first that our people of concern turn to for protection, assistance and counselling.

"Faith-based organisations often enjoy higher levels of trust from the community, better access and broader local knowledge, all of which are important assets in programme design and delivery, including in complex and insecure environments," he concluded.

In his closing remarks to the meeting, he said: "Religion and spirituality motivate and propel individuals, communities and organisations to help those in need and to save them from danger. There was unanimous recognition of the valuable contributions that faith organisations and communities make to the protection of refugees and the displaced.

"The key recommendation that we take away from this discussion is the need for humanitarian actors, including UNHCR, to deepen their understanding of religious traditions across faiths and to become more 'faith literate'. This means a better understanding not only of the central role of faith in the communities we work with, but more concretely of faith structures and networks, and of the different approaches needed for effectively engaging with different types of faith-based actors," he pointed out.

UNAIDS: *Addressing Faith in Action* – a session at the International Conference on AIDS and STIs in Africa held in Cape Town in December 2013, UNAIDS Director, Michel Sidibé, assured FBOs of the crucial role they play: "We can bring billions of dollars but they will not change society, it is your networks and capacities that will bring about change." It is clear that the UN recognise faith-inspired organisations as important agents of transformative change in the world. Missionaries are part of that change.

In their partnership agreements with FBOs, UNAIDS and UNHCR recognise the absolutely critical importance that faith-based values are not compromised in development and humanitarian programmes, that is, their faith is recognised as fundamental to their values and their activities. It is, and will remain, a core principle for Catholic missionaries.

In a special message to Sr. Joan Kirby RSCJ on 19 October 2010, Ban Ki-moon paid tribute to this American sister's work at the UN saying: "I am very pleased that you are receiving a Lifetime Achievement Award for your work at the United Nations on behalf of the Temple of Understanding. We are especially mindful of the special role you have played in advancing the Millennium Development Goals and interfaith and intercultural dialogue, as well as confronting climate change. I am also thankful that you have taken the time to nurture young global citizens from all parts of the world. Your leadership has been exemplary. Your influence profound. I thank you."

Sr. Joan typified many religious – Irish and from around the world – advocating at the UN. This tribute and the positive interface between the UN and religious communities globally should set an example for governments on the importance of faith in public affairs.

II

Consultative Status of Religious at the UN

Many congregations, either as a single entity or as networks, have obtained consultative status at the Economic and Social Council (ECOSOC) of the UN under Article 71 of the Charter of the United Nations. These include the Mercy Sisters, the Religious of the Sacred Heart of Jesus, Presentation Sisters, Daughters of Charity, Loreto Sisters, Franciscans International, Edmund Rice International, VIVAT International, UNANIMA International, Dominican Network, and Augustinians International. For this, a congregation or a network must form an NGO as the link which enables it to contribute the experience, reflection, and analysis of the congregation or the network to the UN.

The active engagement of a congregation, generally working in collaboration with other like-minded groups to maximise influence, is powerful in matters of concern such as the process for agreeing the Strategic Development Goals in 2015 where religious pursued specifically the issues of water and sanitation as the foundations for health, well-being and education of poor people. The basis of this engagement is the experience and wisdom of lived realities in different countries as experienced and relayed by members of the congregation. The congregation's commitment to people existing in poverty, women, migrants and children, lived out in multiple cultural, religious, socio-economic and socio-political settings around the world, is its strength. That strength grown upwards from grassroots level is used at the international level where global action can be taken.

The activities of religious groups at the UN can be summarised as lobbying or responding to ECOSOC, or one of its bodies, that may seek information or advice from religious in their area of expertise; attendance at certain events, conferences, and activities at the UN such as the various Commissions, and submitting written statements on subjects that are relevant to ECOSOC's work and in which religious have a special expertise. Subject to the requirements in ECOSOC Resolution 1996/31, religious can also make oral presentations to ECOSOC.

For input into all of these activities, the NGO representative relies heavily on the members of a congregation to provide reliable and factual information. In other words, active participation from the grassroots in the mission at the UN is indispensable. Currently, there is a number of Irish missionaries engaged as representatives in New York, and in Geneva where the Human Rights Commission is located. Some networks take interns from within congregations as a training and capacity building opportunity for a congregation.

Moved to action by their personal experiences in Africa, three missionary congregations – the Missionaries of Africa, the Congregation of the Holy Spirit (Spiritans), and the Society of African Missions – founded the *Africa Faith and Justice Network* (AFJN) in 1983 to influence United States policy towards Africa. Since that time, membership has grown to over 30 congregations. AFJN works primarily with the executive and legislative branches of the U.S. government to advance its aims, and also has consultative status with the UN. It is an extension of missionary witness in the important arena of U.S. political decisions that affect African people.

At European level, the Africa Europe Faith and Justice Network (AEFJN) was established in 1988 with a presence in Africa and in Europe. With over 50 member congregations, it promotes economic justice between the European Union and sub-Saharan Africa so that the poor of Africa may look forward to a better future. It lobbies and does advocacy at different levels on behalf of African interests.

III

The Role of Religious at the United Nations
Sr. Deirdre Mullan RSM

The sisters and priests who serve as their congregations' delegates to the United Nations are here as the voice and witness to the corporate stance that religious congregations have taken to be prophetic witnesses to justice.

Having a representative at the UN is a very expensive commitment and yet it is a congregation's way of taking Catholic social teaching seriously through advocacy and influencing. The various collective voices of religious men and women, whether at the United Nations during commissions or conferences or when we interact with various bodies, such as UNICEF, is an opportunity to express our radical commitment to Jesus' vision of a way of life lived in solidarity with the poor and oppressed of our world.

The personnel who represent their congregations here, are people of that vision. They know that it is easier to critique the present than to create an alternative future – knowing that such a future is God's work. They bring to the United Nations a quality of soul which sees the presence of God in real life. They see the holy in the suffering of this world and feel compelled to work for a world where no one is excluded.

At the United Nations, religious ask uncomfortable questions because many have lived with and among poor people and so they know first-hand the face of

Sr. Deirdre Mullan RSM and Prof. Joy U. Ogwu, Nigeria Ambassador to the United Nations, who launched the book, It is Good for Us to be Here   *Courtesy Sr. Deirdre Mullan RSM*

suffering, the feel of suffering, and the smell of suffering, and they are able to hone in on the lives of the excluded people of our planet. They speak up and speak out, and are playing a significant role in shaping a more human world. This was particularly evident in the meetings and run-up to agreement on the Sustainable Development Goals in September 2014.

UNICEF – the United Nations children's wing – recognised the quality of the work of individuals here, and so invited me to join for the purpose of seeking ways that they could form effective partnerships with religious on the ground. This work is now in progress.

There are some very large and some very small religious congregations here. Some have formed partnerships, as individual, small congregations could not afford to be here, nor have their voices heard if we were not partnering together, thus enabling all voices to have a place at the table. The message of religious is clear and direct. Many recognise in the words of Pope Francis: "Consumerism is faceless; it is without conscience and unrestrained by anything other than its own materialistic dynamics, and thus it is incapable of having moral responsibility."

Individually and collectively, the congregations who make up Religious at the United Nations (RUN) passionately believe that together we can transform this behemoth called injustice. By recognising the right of every person to life, in a safe environment and world where all indeed will have enough, we keep each other on track, especially when we are tempted to promote ourselves rather than the mission of Jesus!

If we were ever to engage radically with the humanitarian and ethical vision of Jesus, it is at the United Nations, or indeed with UNICEF, where the heartbeat of nations is monitored. It is here that governments meet as equals and are called to be moral agents with responsibility for the common good. We are here to make sure that government representative and UN agencies are people of their word! As we face the future together, it is with the realisation that we as a species have violated planetary boundaries, and we are left with the life and death question: Can there be progress at the cost of survival itself?

Speaking at the *World Economic Forum* in Davos, Switzerland on 29 January 2009 about the role of NGOs at the UN, Secretary General, Ban Ki-moon said: "Our times demand a new definition of cooperation – governments, the private sector and civil society working together for the collective global good." We are at a great moment of transformation; there is a sense that we are on the brink of a future that is at once known and unknown, linked to our present experience, yet beyond and different from it. Will we have the courage to grasp it? Or will we continue with business as usual, oblivious to the mayhem around us?

Our members, who work on the ground with the poorest of the poor, see the UN as the greatest talk show in the world! And our members and critics have a point. If the collective good is indeed the focus of the UN, then the organisation must urgently reform its structure in order to stay relevant in a world facing unprecedented conflicts. The UN's self-inflicted wounds have not done the organisation any favours and yet, for all its indignities, the organisation has helped colonised peoples in the developing world achieve their independence, causing UN membership to nearly quadruple from 51 to 197 member states since its founding in 1955.

The UN is the embodiment of the 'world's conscience' because it is the place where governments assemble to enshrine their legal and moral commitments. It is the home of international rules which, if followed, would breed greater peace and security. And yet for all its faults and failings, the UN and its children's agency – UNICEF – provides food every day for 118 million people in 75 countries; vaccinates 40% of the world's children, saving 2 million lives each year. It assists 40 million refugees and others fleeing war, famine and persecution; fights climate change and leads international efforts in the wake of natural disasters.

Anthony Lake, CEO of UNICEF recognised the contribution of religious when he said: "Long before there was a UNICEF, women and men religious were on the ground meeting the needs of some of the world's poorest and most vulnerable children."

What inspires each of us is different, and yet what keeps us focused is the vision of a world where no one is excluded, knowing that God has promised to be with us, to see things through with us – to be the conscience of our world. This is our justification for being at the UN – to be the conscience of the world in solidarity with the poor and the marginalised.

Sr. Deirdre Mullan is a Sister of Mercy from Derry in Ireland. She holds a Ph.D in the Feminisation of Poverty and how systems affect women and girls worldwide. Currently, she works with UNICEF identifying ways in which this UN body can work more closely in partnership with religious on the ground.

It is Good for Us to be Here details Catholic
religious institutes as NGOs at the UN.
Fr. Emeka Xris Obiezu OSA

IV

What Does a Missionary Perspective Offer Human Rights?
Susan Cahill

In June 2011, I walked the violent slums of El Mezquital in Guatemala City with Fr. Gerry Moore OFM. At the time I was producing a radio documentary on violence against women in Central America. That short walk changed how I understand human rights. It opened my eyes to two important realities. The systematic patterns of injustice in our world today and the complex field of human rights and social justice work. When I got home to Dublin, I realised my time with Fr. Gerry had fundamentally challenged my perceptions of the role of faith-based values in development work. Fr. Gerry surprised me. I left Guatemala with a broader perspective on human rights. Within a few months I enrolled for a Masters in International Human Rights Law at the Irish Centre for Human Rights, NUI Galway.

When thinking where to begin writing this article on my direct experience of human rights and social justice work by Irish missionaries, I immediately thought of Fr. Gearoid O'Connaire O.F.M. When I first met Fr. Gearoid in 2010, I was researching the work of the Irish Franciscan Province in El Salvador. Fr. Gearoid was hugely helpful and patient. The first time we met, he welcomed me with open arms and with the surprising words "the work of missionaries is to do themselves out of a job." I have to say I was little taken back by his frankness. He was not what I was expecting. But then what was I expecting? Fr. Gearoid listened. He explained to me: "Action without contemplation tends to be ego driven" and highlighted "how improvements in human rights cannot be achieved purely by legal mechanisms, but needs to include a growth in spiritual consciousness and sustainable systems for all life forms." His words were refreshing, inspiring, but most of all sincere.

Working in journalism you meet lots of influential personalities. Some amaze, others disappoint. In 2015, I travelled to Haiti and the Dominican Republic with the support of Misean Cara to produce a documentary on the issue of statelessness in the Dominican Republic. Travelling through the Dominican Republic I realised that it is very easy to get lost in all the political and legal debates and forget about the people behind the story. The people who matter!

Then I met with Fr. Marino Serrano SJ, the Director of the Jesuit Refugee Service in Jimani, a small, poor chaotic frontier town on the border between Haiti and the Dominican Republic. Sitting in a noisy, dusty car park in the blazing heat, Fr. Marino explained to me how his faith compels him and other Jesuits to speak up for the rights of men, women and children who are dehumanised by institutional discrimination. Within three minutes Fr. Serrano had crystallised everything that I had learned in NUI Galway. He demonstrated the importance of global solidarity. How did he do it? By introducing me to the face of human suffering! To Maria, a bright 21-year-old Dominican girl of Haitian descent who was stateless. Maria's story was heart breaking. In an instant I learned about the relationship between faith, hope and suffering. Something I could only learn by coming close to those who face injustice.

Documentary making opens up the world to you. But it can also throw you into some very challenging and difficult situations. Over the years I have met and interviewed missionaries who think nothing of their personal safety. In Mozambique, Haiti, Liberia, El Salvador, Venezuela, Bolivia, Vietnam, South Africa, India, Uganda and Colombia I have been humbled by the courage, commitment and energy of Irish missionaries and their colleagues and supporters who are speaking out against systematic human rights abuses, political corruption, environmental degradation, impunity and greed.

One such human rights advocate is Sr. Áine O Connor RSM, who was the Mercy Global Action Coordinator at the UN in New York for some years. On one of her visits to Dublin, we were talking about the global water crisis and environmental degradation, when out of nowhere Sr. Áine blurted the words of Fr. William Reiser, SJ: "To hear God's word, listen to the world." I asked her what she meant by that. She smiled and told me: "We join the dots. We journey with the people and the earth." Sr. Áine was one of several religious who advocate for human rights and social justice at the UN where congregations have consultative status.

Today a lot of human rights defenders question whether religion helps or hinders development. My documentary work with Irish missionaries has taught me that faith is not an obstacle to development and that human rights starts and ends with human values. Meeting and getting to know many inspirational missionaries over the years has inspired me as a journalist and as a human being to challenge the systemic patterns of inequality and where possible, to speak truth to power. It has been a privilege and eye opener. It has reminded me that grace, humility and courage are possible even in the most difficult of situations. It has challenged my weaknesses and my prejudices.

Without doubt Irish missionaries and human rights defenders are living through massive social and cultural upheaval. Social media is giving voice to victims of human rights violations. Ireland is becoming a more secularised society. New generations of lay missionaries like Gena Hearty, the Director of *Nos Petites Freres et Soeurs*, in Kenscoff, Haiti are successfully carrying forward the legacy of Irish missionaries side by side with local missionaries in developing countries. In 2015, I visited Gena in Haiti and asked about her personal and spiritual mission. She replied: "To be a person of love."

A couple of weeks ago I was researching the human rights situation in Honduras for an upcoming documentary I am producing on the issue of impunity. As I was reading through a series of reports on the appalling human rights situation in the country, I began to feel very despondent. I began wondering if human rights treaties and norms actually influence the behaviour of governments. All the reports I was reading pointed to two stark realities – the lack of accountability, integrity and transparency in our global political and economic systems, and the increasing vulnerability of human rights defenders.

I wondered how would some of the missionaries I have met across Africa, Asia and Latin America make sense of all this suffering. Fr. Gerry came into mind. From those boarded-up windows and barbed-wire fences in Guatemala City, I learned that grace empowers humanity. I learned why laughter is important. I learned how human values such as dignity, respect, compassion, solidarity and friendship support long term healing, hope and transformation. I realised that human rights abuses cannot be solved through legal frameworks alone. That it also takes values, belief, vision, courage and love.

Susan Cahill is the presenter and producer of 'Talking Books' on Newstalk Radio and the producer of 'Talking History' programme. She has produced over twenty documentaries for Newstalk on human rights and social justice issues. She holds a Masters in International Human Rights Law from NUI Galway.

V

The Learning Experience of One Missionary at the UN

UNANIMA International – a network of 21 congregations – takes interns in its offices at the UN in New York in order to give them experience and training as well as extending its sphere of influence. Sri Lankan intern and Sister of the Divine Saviour, Sr. Amila Rodrigo SDS reflected on her experience and learning in an insightful article in the organisation's newsletter in January 2016. This was her reflection:

"My experience with UNANIMA International has given me life and hope, and helped me to feel closer to millions of people who struggle to live a dignified life, preserving its sacredness in spite of all violence, war, and destructive forces that surround them. I am proud that my religious congregation is a member of UNANIMA. As an intern, I had access to important UN bodies like the Security

Council, the General Assembly, the UN Committee sessions and many NGO meetings. I met many dedicated people who selflessly serve the most needy and vulnerable.

"I have learned more about human rights, people living in poverty, violence against children and women, women and environment, climate change, human trafficking, migrants and refugees, people with disabilities, indigenous issues, peace, security, drinking water/sanitation, and other issues in social development. Participating in the UN Third Committee, I have experienced in depth the reality of our world – its brokenness and its hopes.

"As I go back to my life and work in Sri Lanka, I will live and work with many victims of the last tsunami. They have been given houses, but the houses do not belong to them. Having homes, they feel homeless because they do not have the property rights to them. Uprooted from their lands, unemployed, they live in extreme material, psychological, and spiritual poverty. Disintegration and hopelessness is their reality. They feel 'left behind'. I believe that there is hope even in the most hopeless place, and I will do all that I can to make the saying 'we leave no one behind' come true in the reality of my people."

"Years ago, Dag Hammarskjöld (as UN Secretary General) said: 'The UN was not created to take mankind to heaven, but to save humanity from hell…' He was right, and that is the UN's mission. It is our mission, too: we are all responsible and co-responsible for our future, for sustainable development, work for human rights, global awareness, education and the interrelationship of all nations. We are all challenged to empower the powerless, to be voice for the voiceless, and to be hope for the hopeless."

Undoubtedly, many other missionaries could equally point to people who have been "left behind" and the challenges they face in responding with solutions.

VI
It is Natural for Missionaries to Contribute at the UN

The work of religious at the UN is becoming a topic for research by scholars and writers. Nigerian-born Augustinian priest, Fr. Emeka Obiezu with others published a book *It Is Good for Us to Be Here: Catholic Religious Institutes as NGOs at the United Nations* in November 2015. Launching the book, Nigeria Ambassador to the United Nations, Prof. Joy U. Ogwu commended the advocacy work of religious at the UN in these words:

"This book, *It Is Good for Us to Be Here*, epitomises the unique advocacy work of organised trans-national actors underscoring the nexus between faith life and working for social development. NGOs of institutes of religious life have been the most influential faith-based NGOs at the United Nations. They have not only played a range of positive roles, but have also affected UN decision-making and its approach to global issues by the moral and ethical consciousness they bring to the entire process of peace, security, and development. Perhaps it is through such a range of positive roles that we can truly beat our 'swords into ploughshares.'"

It is natural for Irish missionaries to make a significant contribution within the UN network in a new form of education and advocacy. Their legacy in formal education is immeasurable as we saw on page 20. An extensive study of the contribution of Irish people to education globally was carried out by the late Dr. Daniel Murphy, lecturer in education at Trinity College Dublin and published in 2000 by Four Courts Press in a 574-page book entitled *A History of Irish Emigrant and Missionary Education*.

Dr. Murphy states: "The most fundamental impact of the mission schools lay in the cultural advancement of the people of Nigeria … What can be claimed beyond any doubt is their cultural empowerment of the primitive peoples of that country through the provision of elementary and secondary education at a time when the colonial authorities failed completely to do so … In particular, they made a significant contribution to the advancement of African women through the large numbers of schools that they founded specifically for girls and staffed by female religious orders."

He points out that a remarkable feature of the Catholic schools throughout South Africa in the nineteenth century was the welcome extended to Protestant pupils. Illustrating the lasting strategic impact of mission schools in Tanzania, he says that that country's first president, Julius Nyerere, "repeatedly acknowledged the country's debt to the missionaries in the field of education and recognised that the dramatic developments he enacted in the course of his twenty-five year rule were largely built on the foundations of the mission school system. His writings clearly confirm his belief that the drive towards universal education of the post-independence period was continuous with a process of cultural liberation initially set in motion by the missionaries."

This education legacy features across the Global South. Dr. Murphy states that the missions had made a notable contribution to education in China during their relatively short stay in the country before their expulsion in 1949. He goes on to say: "The mission schools made an important contribution to the education of the Filipino people in the years when provision of education was entirely inadequate for its large population."

Chapter Eight

Local Missionaries and Religious Step into Irish Shoes

As we have seen in earlier chapters, missionaries are people who are sent or received. They plant seeds of vocation wherever they go. The intention of mission is not that a missionary should stay in the same place for ever. Their key task is to empower the local community in building the local church and helping them to become self-sustainable and in charge of their own mission which is about the Kingdom of God. The entire Catholic Church is missionary which is a never ending activity. In *Redemptoris Missio* (33), Pope John Paul II explained that although the whole church is missionary, not all mission is to be classified in the same way and he used the notion of different situations calling for different forms of missionary activity.

Although missionaries engage in a lot of development and humanitarian work – a central element of Christianity – their deep faith and expression of mission as their motivation makes their work different to that of career secular development workers.

Missionary congregations and societies in Ireland and Europe have been in transition for many years as the number of new entrants to them declined. That change did not take them by surprise. They understand transition as intrinsic to their faith. The Superior General of the Spiritans in his report to their general chapter meeting at Itaici in Brazil in 1992 pointed out: "In the years ahead, the multicultural character of the communities is going to change. This is a challenge which the congregation is called upon to confront at the end of four centuries of its existence." The congregation's general council meeting at Knechtsteden in Germany in 1978, referring to international teams, said that their "new style are of recent origin ... typical of the requirements of missions today and tomorrow ... this is the style of Spiritan missionary commitment in the years to come."

The understanding of mission has changed too, and not just as a consequence of the Second Vatican Council. "Mission is not only reaching out to others but the greater mission of today is reaching in and being personally challenged to reflect and become aware of the world around. Missionaries were seen as the great explorers who dedicated their lives in learning the language of the people we serve, been challenged socially and politically to respond to the marginalised, but as the world is in a process of change and challenge, our mission is challenging and changing." These were the words of Fr. P.J. Cassidy, a Missionary of Africa, in his homily at the RTE televised Mass on Mission Sunday in October 2015.

Over the decades Irish missionaries reached out in extraordinary large numbers to communities in developing countries. That was a particular phase in the missionary cycle. The current phase is about those in the south "reaching in and being personally challenged to reflect and become aware of the world around." Many congregations are enjoying a plentiful supply of vocations in countries in the Global South. The US author and journalist John Allen referred to the Philippines, India, Nigeria and South Korea last year as "the PINS of 21st century Catholicism" because of the numbers of missionaries they are sending to other countries. For example, South Korea has over 1,000 missionaries ministering in developing countries. It has almost 5,000 priests active in ministry nationally with just 138 foreign priests, and an average of 150 men being ordained each year.

Sr. Louis Marie O'Connor of the Sisters of St. Joseph of Cluny ministered for decades in Sierra Leone. Reflecting on the congregation's celebration of their 150th anniversary in January 2016 she said: "I was there for the 100th anniversary and the place has changed so much since then. In 1956 we had no local sisters, and I clearly remember opening the door one day to a local girl who wanted to join. That was the beginning of profound change. She was professed in 1962. It is such a joy and a blessing to see how things have changed, and now the congregation is almost all local sisters – a positive development that fills me with pride and hope.

Sr Beatrice Magaya RSHM, Sr Pamala Penkert RSHM, and Sr Kay O'Neill FMDM taking a break during the Mission Today & Tomorrow Conference in 2013   *Irish Catholic*

"We have empowered other people and that is the essence of mission ... what missionaries are all about ... to work ourselves out of a job. Today, I see a great future for the Catholic Church in Sierra Leone which is almost self-sufficient with vocations. Our task has been completed, but the fulfilment and the joy is that the work continues in a new and vibrant phase with local people serving their own communities with the same Christian values as part of the universal church. However, in such a very poorly developed country, they will continue to need material support and encouragement from Ireland," she concluded.

Writing in the IMU newsletter in December 2014 also about Sierra Leone, Irish Spiritan priest, Fr. Brian Starken gave a similar insight into the church there: "Having first gone to Sierra Leone in 1975 when the Sierra Leonean Church was completely dominated by ex-patriot missionaries, it is fair to say that 40 years later the face of the church has changed completely. In 1975 there were just four local clergy – today you have a church that, in terms of personnel, is largely self sufficient. The vast majority of parishes are run by local priests, and the senior seminary and a number of third level educational institutions are served by well qualified Sierra Leonean staff. The church today is certainly more Sierra Leonean – not just in terms of personnel but also in terms of liturgical enculturation and the involvement of laity in the life of the parish."

Speaking at the *Mission Today & Tomorrow Conference*, Sierra Leonean-born Sr. Clare Stanley SJC said: "The first and the most important preparation for the future of mission is that Irish missionaries came and planted the seeds of faith, they saw this faith take root and begin to bear fruit. They established the local church. Now it is up to local missionaries to sink the roots deeper and produce ever more fruit." Of course, missionaries from other nations were involved too in establishing the local church in the Global South.

Young men studying for the priesthood in Zambia   *World Missions Ireland*

Currently, the Missionary Sisters of the Holy Rosary have 169 sisters working in Africa, and 93% of them are African. All of their members in Kenya, Ethiopia, Sierra Leone and Nigeria working in education, health, and social and pastoral care are African, whilst 40% of their members in Liberia are African with just one Irish sister working in Zambia. Overall, 47% of the congregation's members are African, 48% are Irish, and 5% are other nationalities. They have 13 sisters on mission in Brazil and Mexico and over one third of them are African – an example of Africa now being a missionary sending continent itself.

The Divine Word Missionaries (often referred to by their Latin acronym, SVD) have been in Ireland since 1939. They came to recruit missionaries for the English speaking parts of the world at first. Their magazine – *The Word* – became synonymous with their presence in Ireland. The printing and distribution of religious cards was another means by which they became known in households all over the country. As a worldwide congregation ministering in 78 countries on all continents, they are today facilitating the training of seminarians from other countries such as China and Germany. In recent years, new missionaries trained in Maynooth have gone to work in Indonesia, Ghana and Argentina.

They are flourishing on other continents. For example, from humble beginnings in Indore in India, they spread out to other states of India where they now have four provinces and one region with nine bishops, 475 priests, 42 brothers and 177 seminarians in vows. Their Kenyan & Tanzanian Province currently has one bishop, 37 priests, four brothers and 18 seminarians. Hundreds of Indian SVDs are today working around the world as missionaries, including two in Ireland.

Fr. Liam Dunne, Mission Secretary of the Irish & British SVD Province describes a recent visit to his colleagues in a number of African countries: "I was very much struck by the witness of our SVD internationality in all the countries that I visited. Everywhere there were mixed communities of young SVDs from India, Indonesia, South America, Europe, the Philippines and of course from different countries of Africa."

"When I visited the parish of Yamumbi in Eldoret, Kenya, I met Gideon Apreku, the parish priest and his assistant, newly ordained, James Mburugu, from Ghana," he added. "They took me on a tour of their parish. Imagine my surprise when, in the sacristy, I found vestments that had been made by the apostolic workers of the Archdiocese of Tuam. This made me aware of a very significant fact that I was to experience many times during my visit. In the past, there had been Irish missionaries in that area, but not now. In so many places young SVDs from all over the world have stepped into the breach. This phenomenon made me appreciate our society so much more," he concluded.

The Society of African Missions (SMA) comprised 760 priests and brothers, now has 228 African-born priests working in three units, each with its own African leadership. They have missionaries in 16 countries that are divided into 11 regions with Irish personnel working in five of them. Ten of the regional superiors are African and one is Polish. Three SMAs are African bishops. The growing diversity of their membership is illustrated in 48 Indian priests, 27 Polish and 12 Filipino. To cater for new seminarians, the SMA has formation houses one each in Poland and the Philippines and three in India, plus 11 in eight African countries. Since their first ordination from these countries in 1991, the massive growth is obvious over the past 25 years. Today, they have about 300 seminarians.

Another example of how mission is being continued in the Global South, is the Sisters of St Louis who were founded in 1842 in France and opened their first house in Monaghan in Ireland in 1959. They currently have missions in Benin, Brazil, France, England, Ethiopia, Ghana, Ireland, Nigeria and the USA involved in education, healthcare, community development and pastoral care.

Superior General, Sr. Winifred Ojo points out: "At present, most of the sisters in Europe and America are retired, while vocations continue to grow in the southern hemisphere especially in Ghana and Nigeria. Each year five or six young women enter the institute to begin their formation training. The missionary work that the sisters started in Africa is being carried on and developed by the Ghanaian and Nigerian sisters, who were trained by the Irish sisters. As well as working in Nigeria and Ghana, some of our African sisters are now on mission in Ethiopia and in a suburb of Paris where there are a lot of immigrants. Our central leadership team which is based in Dublin consists of three African born sisters and one born in the USA."

Today, about 40% of Presentation Brothers are not Irish. The new base of the Patrician Brothers is India where they are receiving new entrants. The Christian Brothers have plans to establish 20 new communities of brothers in the developing world by 2020, and have already set up four of these in western Zambia. Most of the membership will be comprised of brothers from developing countries. Their policy is to research where they are wanted, and then identify needs there where they can empower local people. "The focus of our work is to awaken local communities to their own power to bring about transformation. We see our transformation closely tied to the transformation of these communities" says Br. Declan Power who is based in Lusaka in Zambia as a member of the transition support team for this project called *Our Way into the Future*.

The Christian Brothers set up the Edmund Rice Global Network as a loose network of organisations, groups and individuals across the world seeking to continue the spirit of Edmund Rice who founded the congregation in 1820. In order to open their communities, it is now intended that lay members of this network who are attracted to the charism of Edmund Rice and volunteer to work alongside the brothers and local people for short or longer periods can live in the brothers' community if they wish, or alternatively, live nearby in another house.

The Sisters of Our Lady of Apostles established a province in Ireland in 1931 with responsibility for missions in English speaking Nigeria and Ghana. In 1990, they were in a position to inaugurate a province in Nigeria – a normal practice for many congregations as their mission regions become sustainable and ready for autonomy.

The Sisters of Mercy were founded by Catherine McAuley in Dublin in 1831, and today number about 7,000 women in nine congregations in over 40 countries. The make-up of the Mercy organisation is quite complex in that the nine congregations (some with slightly different names) are autonomous, sharing the same foundress, ethos and charism. The various leaders come together under the umbrella of Mercy International Association based in Dublin. The geographical spread from Ireland with provinces in Great Britain, the Philippines, New Zealand, Australia, Newfoundland and the USA is a remarkable success story in mission showing the vision and influence of Catherine McAuley whose cause for canonisation is well advanced.

The first Irish Mercy sisters landed in South Africa in 1897. Today, there are missions in Nigeria, Kenya, Zambia, South Africa, and Peru. Of the 55 sisters in Kenya, six are Irish; of the 43 in South Africa, 27 are Irish-born, and of the eight in Peru, three are Irish-born.

New models of mission are also being created. Speaking in Dublin in May 2011 at an Irish Aid organised discussion on the future of the Irish missionary movement, Sr. Patricia Murray IBVM spoke of her then role with Solidarity with South Sudan – a collaborative of over 200 religious congregations working in a new structure

Young Holy Rosary Sisters in Nigeria awaiting their missionary assignments   *Holy Rosary Sisters*

for mission. She said that the difference between that venture and those of the past was that the missionaries are already planning their exit strategy. "As you go in, you are preparing to leave," she explained. "We are not bringing God to Sudan, God is already in Sudan. We go knowing we are guests, and we go there learning from the mistakes of the past when we thought we had the answers but didn't" she said. This new model is about helping the people to stand on their own feet, and about the local church and the universal church enriching each other" she added.

Sr. Patricia was reflecting the words of Pope John Paul II who said during his visit to Malawi in May 1989: "I urge you to look inside yourselves. Look to the riches of your own traditions, look to the faith which we are celebrating in this assembly. Here you will find genuine freedom – here you will find Christ who will lead you to the truth." This approach indicates the maturing of the interpretation of mission after Vatican II.

Nigerian missiologist and lecturer, Fr. Francis Anekwe Oborji in a paper – *Towards African Model and New Language of Mission* – written for SEDOS (service of documentation and study of global mission) says: "African churches are said to be among the most lively churches in Christendom today. Besides that, young churches of Africa have started sending their own children as missionaries to many parts of the world. The strength of Christianity in Africa is as a result of the active participation of the laity and their generous contribution to the growth of the Church both locally and internationally."

Some congregations forge partnerships with NGOs to achieve greater impact. For example, the Sisters of Mercy and NGO Vita are collaborating in the delivery of sustainable livelihoods to thousands of farm families in Ethiopia and Eritrea enabling them to be free of aid dependency through a range of integrated projects.

In January 2016, the Religious Sisters of Charity in Ozoro in Nigeria formalised the Friends of the Sisters of Charity as a community-based support group to spread their charism and mission throughout the local community. This congregation also has Friends of Mary Aikenhead (foundress of the congregation) supporting them in other missions such as in Okpara Inland and Festac in Nigeria. These support groups hold the same embrace as missionaries ... an embrace that denotes friendship, love, appreciation, warmth, joy and trust. That embrace conjures up depth of feeling, of concern and availability opening the gates to inclusion, dignity, and healing. In the true Christian spirit, the attitude of indifference or individualism has no place within it.

Local religious and indigenous missionaries who are members of the congregations who sent Irish missionaries in the past, are the central people carrying forward the Irish legacy. A good example is the Daughters of Charity whose sisters from Great

Britain and Ireland ministered in Ethiopia for many years. Today, the leadership of their Ethiopian Province is in the hands of local sisters who continue the work with almost 70 sisters located in 16 houses throughout the country. In 2014, when President Michael D. Higgins and his wife, Sabina, visited the St. Louise Eye Clinic in Mekelle, where Mrs Higgins' sister worked for 23 years, they met the Ethiopian sisters who now manage the clinic.

Sr. Kenyuyfoon Gloria Wirba is a member of the African Province of the Congregation of the Tertiary Sisters of St. Francis of Assisi located in Cameroon. She teaches courses in the theology of consecrated life at the Institute of Catechesis and Missionary Spirituality at the Pontifical Urbaniana University in Rome. Writing in *The Global Sisters' Report* on 12 March 2015 about religious life in Africa she noted: "Many new diocesan institutes are springing up in many places on the continent. These are welcome as they contribute to the fullness of the being and apostolate of the church."

Over the last 30 years the church in the south has achieved significant growth, and there is now a wide network of local structures embedded in communities to partner in development activities. That growth is illustrated by plans for all Catholic dioceses in Kenya to own radio stations by 2020. Bishop Joseph Obanyi, Chairman of the Kenya Conference of Catholic Bishops Commission for Social Communications says: "Our aim is to see spiritual and social transformation of people; we want to see integral transformation of the human person as a result of strong Catholic media presence. This is a demand by the faithful to have their own medium of communication within their reach and also to ensure progressive evangelisation."

Many Catholic dioceses throughout Africa have a development office as part of their infrastructure. This is for planning by the young church to continue the type of community-based development work that Irish and other foreign missionaries introduced in past decades. For example, the Diocese of Kitale in Kenya, established in 1998 with an Irish missionary Bishop Maurice Crowley SPS in charge, has a development office with the following objectives:

"To promote effective co-ordination of community development work in the diocese; to establish and maintain strong and effective linkages with target communities, development partners, diocesan institutions, civil society, and other religious organisations and the government; to promote self-reliance of programmes and communities through effective project management, to enhance even distribution of development projects in the diocese; to facilitate planning, leadership, coordination, monitoring and evaluation of all diocesan development projects, and to improve capacity of diocesan development staff for efficiency in providing services." These objectives illustrate understanding and adherence to good practices in development activities.

Fr. Joseph McGee, Irish Provincial of the Missionaries of the Sacred Heart speaking about their mission in South Africa says: "In many of our parishes the nature of mission has changed in that self-regenerative Catholic communities have developed. All of our parishes enjoy a sound infrastructure, a variant degree of self-sufficiency, a lively ministerial involvement and a range of other programmes that cater for all, from the old to the young. A great shift from clerical to lay involvement in social issues has been encouraged over the years. Poverty relief and a response to HIV /AIDS are now major social features of all our parishes."

Of course, the Zulu Missions in the Archdiocese of Durban have been functioning for many decades, initially under the guidance of Archbishop Denis Hurley (son of an Irish emigrant), and presently under Cardinal Wilfrid Napier who studied in Ireland – both of whom built up a strong base of supporters in Ireland.

The Congregational Leader of the Medical Missionaries of Mary, Sr. Siobhán Corkery, is very positive about the future: "From the beginning Medical Missionaries of Mary was an international congregation of women religious, founded by Marie Martin in Nigeria, in 1937. Her desire was to share Christ's healing love and bring health services to people of different cultures where human need was great. Our first African sister entered MMM in 1953 as a trained nurse/midwife. All of my MMM life I have lived in international communities.

"In the early part of the 20th century many missionary congregations and societies were founded by Irish women and men. While there are reducing numbers of MMMs joining from Europe and North America, I believe that we have a future full of hope. Our very life is mission. The 'mission' transcends any ministry or work. The next generation of MMMs are giving expression to our healing charism in new and creative ways. The mission of MMM will flourish and continue to bring life and healing," she concludes.

Missionary sending ceremony in South Korea *World Missions Ireland*

1

St John of God Brothers in South Korea are now Sending Missionaries
Brother Pio Chang OH

When I first entered the order, there were many Irish brothers working and living in Gwangju. There was also a large Irish Columban missionary presence in the Archdiocese of Gwangju.

Until the brothers started admitting Korean vocations, the social contacts of the brothers were mainly with other Irish missionaries. The life style and daily schedule of the community was 100% Irish, similar to that as observed in the other houses of the Irish Province. However, once the decision was taken to admit Korean vocations, the brothers went out of their way to introduce Korean customs and cultural practices into the life of the community. So, by the time I joined the order, it was a very Korean community including customs, food, and also prayers and the daily conversations were in the Korean language. It cannot have been an easy transition for some of the community.

I was very impressed by the works that had been established by the order. The general clinic, which was opened by the brothers in 1960, met the needs of all who came with special attention always given to the poor and needy, and no one was turned away. A home care-visiting program was established to meet the needs of the housebound and the terminally ill, which eventually evolved into the hospice and home care programme. I was privileged, as I was able to be part of the expansion of the order in Korea, making foundations in other parts of Korea where until then there had only been one house located in Gwangju.

The brothers were always looking for ways to respond to new social needs. This made them and their services very well known in the local community. One brother, who was a psychiatrist, saw the need for a psychiatric service, and they started it in a small way. This evolved into the present psychiatric hospital. These days the WHO, as well as the Korean Government, recognises the hospital as a model service.

The Irish brothers came to Korea to assist the people following the aftermath of the Korean War, and then to establish the order in Korea. One thing that I admired about those brothers was their ability to allow the Korean brothers to develop the order as a Korean entity, and not try to make it into an 'Irish' order in Korea. The development in Korea of a separate independent province of the order worldwide was not due to a decline in the number of Irish brothers but rather due to the encouragement and leadership training given to the Korean brothers during formation by the Irish brothers, as well as the thriving apostolates and continued support given to the Korean province by the Irish province.

Today we have thriving province in Korea which is 100% Korean, but which still feels a strong attachment and respect for the Irish province and appreciation for the commitment that it made to the Korean church.

Continued financial support from Ireland would be appreciated as it would be beneficial to our works in China where the Korean brothers are now working, rather than in Korea where the government is very supportive of the works of the order. Today, the Korean brothers have also become missionaries and are now working in China, Japan, Philippines and Argentina. This spirit is another trait inherited from the Irish brothers.

Br. Pio Chang OH is director of St. John of God projects in Seoul, capital of South Korea. He served as provincial, and spent some time in Ireland.

II
Congregations are Adapting and Transforming to be Relevant in a New Era
Fr. Victor Dunne SPS

Today in our great world, most people are enjoying an improving quality of life and are confidently facing the challenges of modern living. People are also searching for ways to nourish their souls and to satisfy the needs of their spirits. St. Patrick's Missionary Society exists to facilitate the fulfilment of these spiritual and human needs, and does so through the proclamation of the Gospel of Jesus Christ and the formation of Christian communities, especially among the least, last and lost peoples of our world.

Because we live in an ever-changing world with new opportunities, St. Patrick's Society has to adapt and transform itself to be relevant and participative in the lives of people. The Society made an important change in 1993, when the then society leader Fr. Kieran Birmingham and his council initiated the process of internationalisation, a process of converting the society from being mainly mono-cultural and Irish to being multi-cultural and international.

The 2014 society chapter made another step in this development when it recommended that the Central Leadership Team move from Kiltegan in Ireland to Nairobi in Kenya. The leadership team made the move in September 2015. While this relocation affirms the present international character of St. Patrick's Society, it also reminds members of the grace and invitation of being an international society; grace in the new diversity and energy that exists in the society and invitation in the call to engage in the work of forming a missionary society drawn from different cultures but united in its commitment to the mission of the society. In this way the missionary work of St. Patrick's Society continues to grow and to respond to the spiritual and human needs of many peoples in many parts of the world. We continue to have a presence in Ireland, and we appreciate the continued prayers and financial support of the people of Ireland for our work in the Global South.

Fr. Victor Dunne is Society Leader of St. Patrick's Missionary Society.

III

"Their Mission is being continued by us Local Sisters"
Sr. Anne Carbon SSC

Ireland has given the world a gift of wonderful and generous missionaries. My country – the Philippines – is blessed with the Columban missionary presence and committed services for the past 77 years. The earlier years were the most challenging when we needed them most. Their commitment, their availability, generosity and readiness to be with the poor and marginalised people was very inspiring. People saw their undying commitment which inspired young local women to join them and share that same charism, passion and missionary spirit.

The Irish sisters are now getting older, but despite our ageing membership the missionary spirit continues to urge us on to new challenges. They might have physically left the mission, but their mission is being continued by us local sisters from the Philippines, Korea, Hong Kong and South America, maybe, taking a different expression of being on mission with different gifts and creative ways that these young members are offering, but definitely with the same missionary zeal from the spirit of our first sisters. It's like letting the seed that was sown by our first sisters mature.

Having seen the wonderful work to go beyond the boundaries of faith and culture done by the Irish missionaries in my country and elsewhere is very inspiring. I know from experience that their own families and friends were always their generous benefactors. The needs are varied, and it can be challenging to get local funding being a third world country. So, having funding support from Ireland and elsewhere would be a great help.

I was privileged to be the first non-Irish member of the congregation to receive funding from Misean Cara in 2005. Writing the detailed application and the project report was a great learning for me. That experience helped me to see how outside help can make life easier for the most unfortunate whose needs are not being responded to by the local government because of lack of funds. External support allows us to implement sustainable projects that empower local communities.

I hope that the Irish government will continue to support missionaries in countries that most need their help. I thank the Irish missionaries and the government of Ireland for the many years of generous commitment, service and help in my country which has given us a lasting legacy.

Our Columban formation is geared towards formation for life. We are taught how to empower people, engage in networking and finding sustainability in whatever ministries we are in. Gone are the days of managing big institutions. Our younger sisters have many creative ways of being in mission, reaching out and journeying with the poor as they insert themselves into cultures different from theirs. Together with the people, they respond to the needs of the place either by providing religious formation, pastoral skills training for adults and youth leaders, and education to help create much needed social transformation.

Being a missionary congregation whose charism is to go beyond the boundaries of our faith and to respond to the signs of the times, the sisters respond to the different emerging needs around us. With mostly local sisters on the front line mission, we are very aware of the present reality and the urgent need to embrace our current challenges to prioritise places of mission and our commitments, and to find creative ways to keep missionary work to the fore.

Sr. Anne Carbon SSC is a Filipino Columban Sister who has ministered in Peru and is currently a member of her congregation's leadership team.

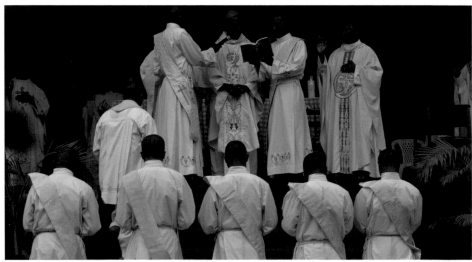

Five SMA priests being ordained in Nigeria in 2015   *Society of African Missions*

IV
Vocations are Plentiful in the East
Sr. Josephine Hong SSC

There are many religious congregations in China, and vocations are flourishing. However, there are many issues arising regarding vocations. The educational background of most of the candidates is elementary school. Some are hoping to receive further education and reach a higher status. The understanding and the meaning of faith is very different which may be due to the huge influence of communism and the importance of money.

The biggest issue is perhaps the lack of experienced sisters and priests who are able to accompany candidates during their discernment. Most of the congregations are under the direct administration of bishops, so the superiors and the formators are appointed by the bishops. Currently, many Chinese religious and priests are studying abroad – some have already returned and more will return to China after their studies. This gives a great hope for the future of Chinese formation.

In China's hierarchy-focused society, 'losing face' or loss of status is regarded as shameful and is taken as an insult both personally and of national pride, so the poor and deprived people are pushed away to the margins of society. Our missionary involvement and contribution to development are greatly needed in China in spite of the country's rapidly growing economy. Our sisters are involved with these people giving them formation and other social and humanitarian support. We appreciate the support we receive from Ireland and other places.

Due to the enormous population, individuals can be slighted and regarded as unimportant and left behind. We are assisting in developing a more humanistic and integrated, holistic approach in social transformation. In this we need both prayer and financial support from Ireland and elsewhere in order to carry out our work within marginalised communities. We pray that this support will continue in the vastness of the tasks that lie ahead of us.

Sr. Josephine Hong SSC is a Columban Sister and a native of South Korea. She has ministered in China, and currently serves on her congregation's leadership team.

V

Mission Cannot be Contained by Geographical Boundaries
Fr. Kevin O'Neill SSC

Ireland has a rich and long history of offering a missionary spirit to the Church and to the world. As far back as St. Columban, 1,400 years ago, who travelled Europe as a missionary pilgrim for Christ, to today, when Ireland opens its doors to welcome the stranger, Ireland is a place of mission in both its sending and receiving missionaries. Where we are called from and where we are sent to is not linear, but rather circular, inviting us always to be missionary and experience mission wherever we are.

Our commitment to inviting and nurturing the missionary vocation we all carry by our baptism is the Columban legacy. In Pope Francis' exhortation, *Joy of the Gospel*, he affirms of mission: "An evangelising community know that the Lord has taken the initiative, he has loved us first, and therefore we can move forward, boldly take the initiative, go out to others, seek those who have fallen away, stand at the cross roads and welcome the outcast" (*Evangelii Gaudium*, No. 24). As such, all mission begins locally, where people can hear God's voice speaking our name in the most intimate way, calling us forth to love and serve, especially where people are vulnerable and creation is wounded.

While the Missionary Society of St. Columban historically began in Ireland, our generalate is now located in Hong Kong. Today and into the future, we see our Columban spirit and identity reflected in a diversity of cultures, races, lay and ordained missionaries. No longer do we see ourselves as exclusively clerical and mono-cultural with mission moving in one direction, but rather as universal towards a future that has unity in our diversity.

The vast majority of our young lay and ordained missionaries, and all our 40 seminarians, are from Asia, Latin America and Oceania. Our commitment to justice, peace, care for creation, dialogue with people of other faiths in intercultural contexts are all ways that we participate in God's mission, calling us forward in communion with our triune God. We believe that mission cannot be contained by geographical boundaries and, as such, place our hope in the movement of the Spirit that is leading us ever more towards a Church that is truly and fully missionary by its nature.

Fr. Kevin O'Neill is Superior General of the Missionary Society of St. Columban.

VI

The Secular World is Noticing the New Generation of Missionaries

On 27 April 2015 Irish Ambassador to Nigeria, Sean Hoy, told a Misean Cara organised meeting of missionaries in Lagos how the cycle of development applies to Irish missionaries. "Irish missionaries," he said "have made a huge contribution to the education of the people of West Africa, most especially in Nigeria. I have visited missionaries who have taught in schools for over fifty years dedicating their whole lives to the education of the future leaders in every sector. I know that this contribution is cherished by the people of Nigeria throughout the country, irrespective of their own religious or ethnic background. In Nigeria, everybody knows Ireland. This is, in no small way, due to the sacrifice and dedication of our missionaries."

He also referred to the new scene with fewer Irish missionaries in developing countries: "We also need to accept that what has worked well in the past will be difficult to replicate as missionary orders are able to send smaller numbers of teachers to Africa. This should be seen as part of the normal cycle of development where teachers can pass on responsibility to their pupils to become the teachers of tomorrow."

Irish Minister of State for Development and Trade, Joe Costello, told the annual general meeting of Misean Cara in June 2012: "The future for the missionaries in Ireland is a challenging one. Religious brothers and sisters of our generation are looking to their African counterparts to take forward the missionary work for the next generation. Fortunately, the church is strongest and at its most vibrant in Africa, Asia, and South America. With challenges come opportunities. There are many young religious in Africa and elsewhere. These young men and women are ready and willing to engage with development processes in their own countries and neighbouring regions. It is important that we continue to support them in seeking solutions to the perennial problems of poverty and inequality."

His theme was taken up by the President of Ireland, Michael D. Higgins in a speech during a state visit to Malawi in November 2014 when he said: "Ireland's original pioneers and ambassadors in Africa were our missionaries, who began to arrive here in Malawi at the beginning of the last century. I am always amazed in my travels by the number of people whose lives have been changed by the education and health services which are the legacy of these selfless, dedicated and committed individuals. The legacy of such people continues today through the inspirational work of their successors here in Malawi and across the globe."

When he visited the Philippines in 2015, journalist and broadcaster Charlie Bird noticed local missionaries doing what their Irish colleagues were doing in past decades. "The one thing that struck me forcefully when I covered the story of 'Negros Nine' all those years ago, was the commitment of the Irish missionaries in the Philippines to the cause of 'social justice' and to be seen to be standing side by side with the oppressed sugar workers on the island of Negros," he said. "This time around I saw a different group of missionaries doing much the same type of work. But for me, one thing that hasn't changed since my first visit to the Philippines is the commitment of missionary priests and nuns to be seen to stand with the people wherever they are working."

Like other observers, he didn't fail to notice the same values and the same type of work being continued by local and indigenous missionaries who are receiving financial support from Ireland through their congregations, Misean Cara and other donors.

The Ambassador of the Republic of Korea, Mae-Yun Park launched the book *Guest from the West*, written by Columban priest, Fr. Hugh McMahon on 21 April, 2015 in Dublin. Referring to the Columban priests in his country he said: "Their contributions to Korea in its most difficult times cannot be underestimated, we cannot thank them enough. This book is a very eloquent and timely read to once again remind us of the valuable contributions of missionaries over the years." Now, in reverse mission, missionaries from South Korea are being sent to other countries in the Global South.

Medical Missionaries of Mary Sisters: Angela Lyapa (Tanzania), Joanne Bierl (USA), and Ekaete Ekop (Nigeria) attending the Mission Today & Tomorrow Conference
Zelie McGrath, Misean Cara

Chapter Nine

Irish Missionaries Founded Local Congregations

A part of the legacy of Irish missionaries that generally goes un-noticed is the local congregations that they founded in Africa and in India, or for whom they provided formation training in the early years. These diocesan congregations are now doing the pastoral and development work that the Irish have done for decades and continue to do but in small numbers.

The pattern in the founding of these congregations was an invitation generally from an Irish missionary bishop in Africa for assistance in the running of his diocese. In 1903, Wicklow-born Sr. Teresa Kearney (later known as Mother Kevin) arrived in Uganda from Mill Hill in London with five Franciscan sisters. In 1923, she founded the Little Sisters of St. Francis of Assisi (LSoSF) who currently have about 600 members.

It 1935 she opened Mount Oliver Convent in Dundalk to receive Irish postulants. Then, in 1952, with growing numbers, she founded the Irish congregation, the Franciscan Missionary Sisters for Africa (FMSA). These two congregations have worked closely together, and in 2003 they celebrated 100 years in Africa. As part of prudent succession planning and empowerment by FMSA, they have handed over many of their schools, hospitals, and leprosarium to LSoSF.

Mother Kevin is greatly remembered in Uganda for her love of the vulnerable and marginalised persons in society, the many schools and hospitals she established, plus her special concern for the care of lepers who were neglected, and her work to raise the status of women and the girl child. When she died in 1957 in the USA, her remains were brought to Ireland for burial. Soon, the cry of her beloved people in Uganda became so great to have her interred amongst them, that she was exhumed and their wish was granted.

Not only is the spirit of Mother Kevin still made manifest through the works of the Little Sisters of St. Francis and the Franciscan Missionary Sisters for Africa, but the President

Gold medal awarded posthumously to Mother Kevin Kearney by the Government of Uganda in 2014   *FMSA Sisters*

of Uganda, Yoweri Museveni named her among the gold medallists during the *52nd Independence* celebration of Uganda held on 9 October 2014 for: "Her contribution towards the development of the country."

That national recognition of her legacy is well deserved when it is considered that today the LSoSF are engaged with medical units in five hospitals in Uganda, three in Kenya, nine dispensaries in Uganda, six in Kenya and one in Tanzania, one community based health centre each in Uganda and Kenya, two nurse training schools, and two leprosorium hospitals in Uganda. They also run seven nursery schools in Kenya, fourteen primary schools in Kenya and twenty-four in Uganda, three secondary schools in Kenya, seven in Uganda, and one in Tanzania, two teaching training colleges each in Kenya and Uganda, two domestic science schools in Uganda and one in Kenya, one special school each in Uganda and Kenya, and have an associate professor and a counsellor working at Kenyatta University. Additionally, they have an extensive social work apostolate.

Mother Kevin was awarded an OBE by the British Government in 1919 in recognition of the work of LSoSF in caring for African soldiers returning from World War 1 in Europe to Kisumu in Kenya.

The Loreto Sisters (Irish branch of the Institute of the Blessed Virgin Mary) founded by Frances Teresa Ball in 1822 sent sisters to India in 1841 where they set up a school. On 26 July 1897 the Congregation of the Daughters of St Anne (Ranchi) was established by Archbishop Paul Goethals, and four girls of Loreto Convent Ranchi were received as postulants, and completed their novitiate and

The Sisters of Mercy Leadership Team in the Philippines in 2015   *Mercy Sisters*

initial formation under Loreto tutelage. This congregation has grown to have 125 houses throughout India.

The Daughters of St Anne (Calcutta) were established in July 1904 by Archbishop Brice Meuleman SJ. They likewise completed their initial formation under Loreto tutelage in Entally and later in Morapi, and the Loreto Indian Provincial was their Chief Superior. Saint Teresa of Calcutta was a member of the Loreto Sisters for 22 years before she set up the Missionary Sisters of Charity in 1950.

In 1949 the Daughters of the Immaculate Heart of Mary were established by Bishop Riegler in South Africa with formation provided by the Loreto Sisters in Glen Cowie. The Loreto Provincial was also leader of this new congregation until 1976 when it elected its own provincial.

Sr. Mary Charles Walker – a member of the Religious Sisters of Charity founded in Ireland – arrived in Nigeria in 1923 at the invitation of Bishop Joseph Shanahan of the Vicariate of Southern Nigeria. Her desire for an indigenous religious congregation was fulfilled when four of the young women she taught in St. Joseph's Convent School in Calabar expressed the desire to become religious sisters. The new congregation – Handmaids of the Holy Child Jesus – was canonically erected in April 1937 by Cavan-born Bishop James Moynagh of the Diocese of Calabar. It became autonomous in 1959 with its own superior general, and today it has convents in Nigeria, Ghana, Cameroon, Togo, Sierra Leone, Kenya, Italy, England, Germany, and North America. Mother Mary moved on mission to Zambia where she died and was buried. The Handmaids were given permission to re-bury her body in Calabar, and are now promoting her canonisation.

In 1937, Irish Spiritan and native of Ballyjamesduff, Co. Cavan Archbishop Charles Heery founded the Congregation of the Sisters of the Immaculate Heart of Mary, Mother of Christ in Nigeria. Their formation training was provided by the MSHRs. "Being a missionary himself he desired that we be missionaries. In the early 1900s women were neglected and excluded from educational and social benefits. Our founder was moved with compassion to the plight of these underprivileged women. This inspired him to found an indigenous women religious congregation that would take care of the needs of women and children. This care should be holistic in nature: educational, social, medical, and spiritual." That is how the congregation describe the values and ethos they inherited from Archbishop Heery who also founded St. Augustine's Teaching Training College in Lavia. The congregation has founded and manages several hospitals and maternity homes. It has missionaries serving in Kenya, Ghana, Sierra Leone, the USA, Canada, the UK plus a house in Rome.

In 1955, Irish Spiritan Archbishop John Joseph McCarthy, a native of Milltown

Malbay, Co. Clare, founded the Assumption Sisters of Nairobi. In 1999, they opened the St. Martin De Porres Teacher Training College which aims to provide graduates with "spiritual formation, skill training and character formation aimed at making them responsible and successful citizens as well as being able to meet the various emerging issues in education." In 2010, Regina Pacis University College, as a constituent college of the Catholic University of Eastern Africa, was opened under sponsorship by the sisters. Its first degree course was Bachelor of Science in Nursing. The sisters aim to assist students from poor socio-economic backgrounds, especially women, to access university education which is too often a dream for students with few or no resources. They have an outreach mission in Jamaica.

Antrim-born Carmelite, Bishop Donal Lamont, founded the Handmaids of Our Lady of Mount Carmel in the Diocese of Mutare in Zimbabwe in 1959. Currently, this diocesan congregation has about 100 members. Bishop Lamont is remembered internationally for his highly influential intervention in the Vatican Council meeting on 12 October 1965 during the discussion on mission and out of which came the Decree, *Ad Gentes*. His closing comment was delivered in Latin at the end of that debate: "No people are so primitive as to be unfit for the gospel; none are so civilised as not to need it," and drew much praise.

In 1960, Irish Capuchin, Bishop Timothy O'Shea, a native of Clondrohid, Co. Cork founded the Little Sisters of St. Francis Livingstone in Zambia. The Franciscan Missionary Sisters for Africa provided early formation training. This diocesan congregation provide a range of pastoral and social services for their own people.

In 1962 the Sisters of the Assumption of Eldoret were founded in Kenya by Kiltegan Bishop Joseph Brendan Houlihan, a native of Ballyferriter, Co. Kerry. Three

The 2011-2014 Leaders of the Association of Consecrated Women in Eastern and Central Africa   *ACWECA*

MSHRs provided formation training for them. Today, they have over 100 members with apostolates in education, pastoral and social care. The Holy Rosary Sisters had been in Ortum since 1956 where they developed Ortum Mission Hospital. In 2014, they transferred its administration to the Sisters of the Assumption of Eldoret.

In 1963 the Congregation of the Sisters of St. Therese of the Child Jesus of Buea were founded by Dutch Mill Hill Missionary, Bishop Jules Peeters in Cameroon, with formation training provided by the MSHRs. Today, the congregation has 60 members and 25 novices and postulants. They minister in five dioceses in Cameroon. Operating from 14 communities, they are matrons, physiotherapists, nurses, pharmacy associates, teachers, instructors, financial associates, and provide pastoral care and rehabilitation to prisoners. They have plans to enter special needs education and to establish a community in Spain.

In 1967 Bishop John Reddington SMA, a native of Athlone, founded Our Lady of Fatima Sisters in the Diocese of Jos in Nigeria. The Irish OLA (Our Lady of Apostles) Province provided formation training for this congregation.

When US-born Archbishop Leo Taylor SMA founded the Eucharistic Hearts of Jesus Sisters in 1943 as the first indigenous congregation in the Archdiocese of Lagos in Nigeria, again the Irish OLA Sisters provided formation. With about 200 sisters currently, these sisters also minister in the USA and Canada.

In 1971, The Sisters of Mary, Mother of the Church in Ho Diocese in Ghana were founded by Dutch-born, Bishop Anthony Konings SMA, with formation training provided by Irish OLA sisters. Today, they are over 80 sisters located in 19 communities engaged in education, health, and social care.

Dublin-born Passionist, Monsignor Urban Murphy CP, Bishop of Gaborone in

Columban Fr. Niall McGill with newly ordained priests in Myanmar   *World Missions Ireland*

Botswana founded the Handmaids of the Sacred Passion of Our Lord Jesus Christ in April 1965 with support from Sr. Consolata Shields, Superioress General of the Sisters of the Cross and Passion. Sr. Olcan Watt and Sr. Martha Burke were appointed for formation training at the novitiate in Lobstse. In 1970, the name of the congregation was changed to the Sisters of Calvary. These two congregations of sisters have worked closely together over the years.

In 1969, Pope Paul VI in his address to the African Bishops in Kampala, Uganda said: "The church in Africa must, in turn, become a missionary church." As we have seen above, this had already begun. In 1977, Cardinal Dominic Ekandem in Nigeria founded the Missionary Society of St. Paul, a congregation of priests that has ordained 266 men including three bishops. St. Patrick's Missionary Society provided formation training for the new congregation in its early years, and initiated and edited its magazine – *The Catholic Ambassador* – until 1991.

In 1986, the members of the Society were sent on foreign missions for the first time to Cameroon, Liberia and the USA. Since then, in addition to these countries and Nigeria, members of the Society now work in Botswana, Gambia, Malawi, Chad, South Africa, South Sudan, Italy, Sweden, Canada, Germany, Grenada and the Bahamas. Thirty of their priests currently minister in the United Kingdom, whilst the Irish church has six with plans to take more.

Writing in *The Catholic Ambassador* in summer 2014, Fr. Stephen Ojapah MSP, who ministers in northern Nigeria, referred to how his congregation can repeat the missionary zeal of the Irish. "Our working conditions are really posing a huge challenge to our mission here. We cover numerous kilometres and hours on the road

During their 200th centenary celebrations in Zambia in 2015, a local Religious Sister of Charity displays an image of their foundress, Cork-born, Mary Aikenhead. When they opened St. Vincent's Hospital in Dublin in 1834, it was the first hospital staffed by nuns in the English-speaking world   *Religious Sisters of Charity*

to get to our churches and reach out to the people of God. The mission here is one of great sacrifice but demands a great deal of financial support and encouragement from the associate members, sponsors and friends of the Missionaries of St. Paul. This is our opportunity to impact positively the lives of Christians here and make their lives worthwhile. We can do in Gidan Mai Kambu what Ireland did for the Nigerian church. We all are beneficiaries of the great missionary sacrifice of the Irish people. Please continue to support our missionary work to bring about God's kingdom. Remember, some give to the mission by going, while others go to the mission by giving," he said.

The Congregation of the Sisters of the Nativity were founded in 1969 by Limerick-born Spiritan, Bishop Donal Murray in the Diocese of Makurdi in Nigeria with inspirational help from Sr. Edith Dynan, then Regional Superior of the MSHRs who provided formation training. Their first overseas mission was to the parish of Cranbourne in the Diocese of Sale in Australia.

In 1971, Limerick-born Jesuit, Bishop James Corboy founded the Sisters of the Holy Spirit in Monze diocese in Zambia. The Religious of the Sacred Heart of Mary sisters from Ireland provided formation training until 1991 which allowed the two congregations to work very closely together. Today, Sisters of the Holy Spirit are involved in work among the poor in schools, hospitals and rural clinics, visiting the sick, caring for the orphaned, assisting families with one or both parents suffering from AIDS. They run the 274 bed Monze Mission Hospital and the 22 bed Chivuna Health Clinic.

Local sisters in Africa are acutely conscious of their need for high levels of education and leadership training in order to be able to lead their congregations. In 2003 sisters from Nigeria, Ghana, Kenya, Tanzania, and Uganda set up *The African Sisters Education Collaborative* that focused initially on computer skills training. Then, in 2007 in collaboration with Marywood University in the USA and 3-year funding from the Conrad Hilton Foundation they formed the Sisters' Leadership Development Initiative to focus on training for leadership skills for women leaders in religious life. The Hilton Foundation provided $5.48 million in 2013 to extend this programme to nine countries to train 756 sisters in leadership and financial management.

Many sisters further their education right up to doctoral level in theology. Sr. Wilhelmina Uhai Tunu, a member of the congregation of the Little Sisters of St. Francis of Assisi speaks highly about the "wonderful programme for training women theologians in Africa where they are few" and says that "their indispensable role is yet to be fully appreciated." Sr. Shalini Mulackal is a Presentation Sister teaching systematic theology at Vidyajyoti College of Theology in New Delhi, and is the President of the Indian Theological Association and a member of Indian

Women Theologians Forum. Like so many others, these sisters are members of Irish-founded congregations who sowed seeds that grew and have borne rich fruit in the Global South.

Female congregations in a number of countries in Africa have formed associations for networking, sharing, and training. The Association of Sisterhoods in Kenya (AOSK) started with 10 congregations in 1962, but on its 50th birthday in 2012 that number had grown to over 150 with 5,200 members. These congregations receive about 250 novices annually. The Zambia Association of Sisterhoods (ZAS) was founded in 1958 with a few congregations and has grown to 47 with a total number of 1,473 women religious of whom 1,022 are indigenous Zambians and 450 are missionary sisters. The Association of Religious in Uganda has 85 member congregations with a membership of around 7,300 religious (men and women) from across the 19 Catholic dioceses of Uganda.

These and similar associations in Eritrea, Ethiopia, Malawi, Republic of Sudan, South Sudan, and Tanzania formed the Association of Consecrated Women in Eastern and Central Africa in 1974. Today, that has a membership of 22,000 sisters which is a vast human resource for great spiritual, pastoral, and development impact in the region. Through these associations, the different religious congregations

Presentation Sister, Shalini Mulackal delivering a theology lecture in New Delhi   *John Mathew*

express their communion which unites them and builds their capacity and their reach.

Globally, female congregations have a worldwide network in the International Union of Superiors General (UISG) that enables them span borders and boundaries in order to create ways for members to be in communication, in community, and in communion. Likewise, male congregations have the Union of Superiors General (USG) for the same purpose of networking and sharing.

In his Apostolic Exhortation – *Ecclesia in Africa* – given at Yaoundé in Cameroon on 14 September 1995, Pope John Paul II recognised the growth of the church in Africa following the 'great missionary epic' especially over the previous two centuries when the continent experienced missionaries from many nations, including Ireland. He said: "The splendid growth and achievements of the Church in Africa are due largely to the heroic and selfless dedication of generations of missionaries. This fact is acknowledged by everyone. The hallowed soil of Africa is truly sown with the tombs of courageous heralds of the Gospel" (No. 35).

"The seed sown at that time has borne much fruit," he added. "My brothers in the Episcopate, who are sons of the peoples of Africa, are eloquent witnesses to this. Together with their priests, they now carry on their shoulders the major part of the work of evangelisation. Signs of this fruitfulness are also the many sons and daughters of Africa who enter the older missionary congregations or the new institutes founded on African soil, taking into their own hands the torch of total consecration to the service of God and the Gospel" (No. 38).

Referring to the missionary nature of the young African church he said: "The missionary institutes founded in Africa have grown in number, and have begun to supply missionaries not only for the countries of the continent but also for other areas of the world" (No. 38).

Recognising the importance of culture in faith, the Pope noted that Africa "is endowed with a wealth of cultural values and priceless human qualities which it can offer to the churches and to humanity as a whole" (No. 42).

The Irish missionaries have made a very significant contribution to Catholic Church structures and religious life formation in Africa. This is an important part of their legacy that is being continued by young and vibrant missionaries there and elsewhere in the Global South.

Chapter Ten

Community Structures to Plan for Their Succession

One means that some missionaries use to plan for the continuation of their social and development work is the setting up of local community organisations that will succeed their own involvement in programmes. This is a highly successful method of leadership and empowerment of local people that brings about sustainable livelihoods and social and economic development that is appropriate in local circumstances, and which can evolve over time, depending on needs and resources available or attainable.

A good example of such a community organisation is the Women and Children First Organisation (WACFO) set up by the Sisters of the Sacred Hearts of Jesus and Mary (SSHJM) in Pabo in Northern Uganda. It is a local initiative in environmental management embracing livelihood and economic security, plus early childhood education including special needs, and a physiotherapy community based rehabilitation project for children and young adults with disabilities in 14 very remote villages where other development actors do not operate.

This pioneering work involves natural resource management by introducing initiatives such as the harvesting of 'run-off' rainwater, the use of indigenous micro organisms for fish and pig feeds, briquette making from waste material as a domestic fuel to replace charcoal, the use of energy saving stoves, fish farming, and underground water utilisation for dry season vegetable production and normal season crop production. The focus is on sustainability that is linked to natural resources and local needs in a very remote and poor rural area. WACFO was ahead of the SDGs and climate change initiatives by the UN in 2015.

Sr. Mary Costello SSHJM is very clear about the objective: "WACFO's overall goal," she says "is to continue opening up windows of opportunity for some of the poorest categories of households living in Pabo Sub-County with the intention of empowering and enabling them to provide for their own basic needs in health, education, nutrition and shelter in the belief that at the centre of sustainable development is the human person; the recognition of the rights of all children, and the specific needs of children with disabilities."

The local administrator of the Pabo Sub-county local government points out: "The involvement of WACFO, and being close to the sub-county local government that is mandated to deliver social services for citizens, will contribute immensely to the success of the organisation's goals and the sustainability of the project in Pabo

Sub-county."

Another example of this strategy for people empowerment is in Latin America. During the El Salvador civil war in 1981, more than 1,000 villagers, mostly women and children, were murdered by the Salvadoran army. El Mozote is known around the world as one of the largest and bloodiest massacres to have been committed in Latin America. The Sisters of the Sacred Hearts of Jesus and Mary have been in El Salvador for 25 years and have worked for 11 years with the survivors and families of the victims of the massacre where the local community struggled for justice for many years.

The survivors were met with indifference by the authorities until the sisters mobilised them by forming the Promotion of Human Rights Association El Mozote to advise and teach them about the legal process to advance their case. This has had success with the Inter-American Court of Human Rights issuing a sentence in 2012 involving a programme of reparations in the areas of education, health care, psychological treatment, housing, infrastructure, monuments, care of the elderly and a register of the victims. The Human Rights Association with oversight from the sisters and others continues to accompany the victims and their families on their journey

María Dorila Márquez de Márquez is President of the Promotion of Human Rights Association. Here she acknowledges the success of setting up the association: "The organisation was founded, and has obtained legal capacity thanks to the support from the Sisters of the Sacred Hearts of Jesus and Mary funded by Misean Cara. From the projects, I have received many benefits on a personal level, such as human rights training and psycho-social assistance that has helped me overcome many obstacles.

"On a community level, thanks to having the association legalised, we have had the opportunity to open a dialogue with different governmental departments, through which we have obtained improvements to the existing monument in remembrance of the victims of the massacre; and in the area of family health we now have a team of community health professionals working with the local population and our families.

"In addition, there are many projects planned for the future of our town, and that of the other affected communities, such as, improvements to education, health, and the preservation of a memorial history. It has not been an easy process for us to achieve these goals, for that, the help of the support team has been important because they are people who we can consult in the process of making informed decisions and who have always been there to accompany us.

"Given that we are not fortunate enough to have the necessary resources to pay salaries, the projects funded by Misean Cara have been a blessing and continue to be of great value to us in the struggle that, little by little, is being recognised in our country, but as yet has many issues that remain unresolved."

In Brazil the Irish Spiritans set up Movimento da Defensa Favelada (MDF) in Sao Paulo to support slum dwellers. It is grounded in the principles of presence, resistance, and solidarity, and works with over 5,000 people in 50 urban slums. Its activities include the training of community leaders and the setting up of local committees in the slums so that they can campaign for their right to decent living conditions. The organisation grew out of prayer meetings where people had opportunities to listen and gain the confidence to discuss issues ... good development starts with conversation and dialogue.

Fr. Patrick Clarke CSSp told Cathal Barry in an interview with *The Irish Catholic* in November 2013 that: "The idea was to help people become empowered and let them gradually make the changes that were appropriate and necessary for their own lives. MDF grew from there."

Sr. Anne Griffin SSHJM (right) with some of the families of the victims of the massacre at El Mozote meet President Higgins and Minister of State for Development, Joe Costello, (left) during a state visit to El Salvador in 2013   *Fennell Photography, courtesy Áras an Uachtaráin*

Youth Alive Uganda was started in 1993 by a group of youth under the guidance of Sr. Dr. Miriam Duggan FMSA in Kamwokya, a suburb in Kampala which was severely affected by a diversity of social and health problems, but chiefly HIV/AIDS. The group realised that the most infected and affected were young people, mainly adolescents and young adults. In response, a youth friendly HIV prevention strategy grounded in behaviour change approaches was designed resulting in the foundation of Youth Alive Uganda. Starting as a peer support group, the long term vision was about fullness of life amidst and beyond the AIDS pandemic, and the imparting of relevant knowledge, life skills, and values that contribute to a positive and healthy society.

The effectiveness of the programme was quickly recognised by the government of Uganda, and Sr. Miriam was appointed to the Uganda AIDS Commission. Youth Alive was registered as an NGO in 1995 and has since spread to 21 African countries. Sr. Miriam's work in this area has been recognised internationally, including by the governments of Ireland and Uganda, and by universities in Ireland and the USA.

Education for Life Kenya is a registered trust organisation that started from a programme devised by Sr. Kay Lawlor MMM for HIV prevention using the counseling process, and which was deepened and expanded by Sr. Miriam Duggan FMSA. Since the 1990s it offers ten programmes based on change management models that can be adapted for different groups. It has 26 independent satellite teams throughout Kenya, and has provided training for facilitators in five African countries. I have experienced parishes in South Africa adopting the programme with very positive impact.

When Sr. Dr. Mona Tyndall MSHR was expelled from Nigeria during the Biafran war she moved to Zambia, first in the Monze mission hospital, and later in Lusaka University Teaching Hospital (UTH). Concerned with hospital overcrowding and high post-natal mortality, she strove to reduce maternal mortality by half in the 1990s in accordance with the *Health for All Alma Ata Declaration*. In this, she was strongly supported by the government of Zambia, and attracted funding from Ireland's overseas aid programme. She helped establish the first ten maternal health clinics, and the country's first related ambulance service. Overcrowding at UTH was substantially reduced, and the project was expanded throughout Zambia where her legacy lives on.

The People's Recovery Empowerment and Development Assistance (PREDA) foundation was founded in the Philippines in 1974 by Irish Columban, Fr. Shay Cullen. It is a social development organisation employing 63 Filipino professionals that implements projects to save children from sexual abusers, and from life in the brothels and sex bars frequented by Filipino men and foreigners of all nationalities.

It saves children from jails and detention centres and gives them a new life of dignity and self-esteem. It advocates for human rights and educates communities. PREDA has been nominated three times for the Nobel Peace Prize and has received the German and Italian human rights awards, and is an international recognised human rights and child rights advocacy organisation.

Fr. Patrick Devine SMA founded The Shalom Center for Conflict Resolution and Reconciliation in Kenya in 2009. Shalom pursues lasting peace by producing the empirical research of the root causes of each conflict, teaching conflict resolution and building inter-tribal trust and cooperation. It holds workshops, trains tribal leaders in conflict resolution, and encourages sustainable human development, for example, through the building of schools powered by solar energy in remote areas historically troubled by violence. The organisation sets out to tackle the root causes, as distinct from just dealing with the symptoms of conflict by having a qualified international team of peace practitioners, from within and outside Africa, who have a vocational commitment to conflict transformation. It operates through partnerships with governments and church and academic structures internationally.

These examples of community-led and other organisations that enable local empowerment of communities demonstrate the enterprise and initiative of missionaries in promoting community ownership and sustainability. They illustrate solidarity, participation, and subsidiarity in action by missionaries as core principles of their ministry and its continuation past their own involvement.

The Paris Declaration on Aid Effectiveness (OECD 2005) and *The Accra Agenda for Action* (OECD 2008) applies not just to countries but at every level. Missionaries use a theory of change that increases community ownership, and allows communities to set the priorities and lead the processes of their own development. Donor agencies should play a supporting role as set out in the Paris Declaration.

These community structures are part of the missionary legacy too. They are grounded in similar strategies used in the setting up of structures in Ireland such as Sophia Housing Association, Respond Housing Association, Focus Ireland, Fr. Peter McVerry Trust and Depaul Housing, and so many others across sectors, including social finance such as Clann Credo Ltd., inspired by the Presentation Sisters.

Some congregations enlist lay involvement to assist their work internationally. For example, the Society of African Missions set up Friends of Africa in 1998 as a registered charity. Many of its members have been volunteers in Africa. The Irish Redemptorists set up SERVE in 2003 as a development and volunteering organisation that is now governed by its own board. The Medical Missionaries of Mary Lay Associates can be found in 16 countries, and they publish their own newsletter for networking. MMM Congregational Leader, Sr. Siobhán Corkery says, "The MMM associate movement has become a strong force for good. The understanding and lived expression of our charism among them continues to be inspiring." Many other congregations have well established lay volunteering programmes of various durations.

These examples are just some of the community-based organisations and programme structures that are part of the Irish missionary legacy, and which will carry forward that legacy for future generations.

Fr. Patrick Devine SMA, Executive Director, The Shalom Center for Conflict Resolution and Reconciliation with Professor Hastings Donnan, Director, Institute for the Study of Conflict Transformation and Social Justice at Queen's University, Belfast. The two organisations have signed a memorandum of understanding which aims to enhance their ability to undertake research into conflict transformation and reconciliation   *Shalom Center*

Chapter Eleven

The Contribution to Mission by Lay People and Volunteers

Some give by going; others go by giving

The Irish missionary phenomenon was described in earlier chapters as a 'movement'. One group of participants who are often forgotten about in describing the movement, are the hundreds of thousands of lay people who engage actively in supporting missionaries – Irish and non-Irish – through their prayers and material or financial support. Most of that support is given directly to congregations through donations, fundraising events, legacies, and Mass offerings. This support enables missionaries to undertake their work with poor communities in developing countries.

Long before APSO or Ireland's overseas aid programmes were contemplated, many congregations set up structures to engage the Irish public in the movement. For example, the Missionaries of the Sacred Heart set up the MSC Mission Support Centre in Cork in 1964 to support their missions. The centre creates friends throughout Ireland and the UK with many of these friendships lasting a lifetime and continuing down through the next generation. The support of these lay people for the missions illustrates the extent of the 'missionary movement' of which they were and remain a pivotal part.

Again, long before development education was a topic for discussion in Ireland,

Sunday school in a parish administered by the Jesuits in Dodoma, Tanzania   *Lucy Franks*

missionaries were using Catholic churches to talk about their work to worshipping congregations. For many decades, the IMU has been organising the parish promotion programme within dioceses. A congregation or a number of congregations are allocated a diocese or part of a diocese within which to appeal to Mass goers for their prayerful and financial support. As was indicated earlier, knowledge about the 'third world' was received by the Irish people through this medium.

Apostolic Workers have been a feature of lay mission involvement throughout Ireland since 1923. Whilst smaller in numbers now, this group of ladies raised almost €1 million in 2014 for the missions. "Our provision of materials, vestments, sacred vessels, funding for churches, education and medical aid, among other things could not be achieved without the dedication and commitment of our members. The time taken to fundraise via church gate collections, sponsored walks, sales of works and other methods allows us to continue to support the important work carried out by the many missionary priests and sisters around the world," says their president, Anne Donaghy.

World Missions Ireland – part of the global Pontifical Mission Societies – is the official mission charity in Ireland that is well known for promoting October as mission month. In addition to engagement with schools, its main fundraising activity is a national collection taken up at Masses on Mission Sunday. In 2014, this raised €1.8 million for distribution to young churches in the Global South.

Ireland is one of 20 countries that has an active branch of Aid to the Church in Need – a Pontifical Foundation – that offers support to persecuted and poverty stricken Christians around the world using local church structures. On average it supports 5,000 projects in 130 countries annually. In 2014, the Irish branch fundraised almost €3 million from the Irish public, putting Irish donations in 12th place out of the 20 countries. Despite the recessionary times and the difficulties faced by the Catholic Church in Ireland, this amount was a significant increase on the previous year.

Recognising that Trócaire raised €23 million from the public for its development work in 2014/15, the level of missionary fundraising – €5.8 million by these three groups alone in 2014 – demonstrates the extent of the engagement with missionary activity by lay people in Ireland. Many more millions are fundraised by congregations directly from their dedicated and loyal supporters and friends around Ireland. This is clear evidence of the extent of the missionary movement in Ireland, and how missionaries and young churches in poor countries continue to benefit from the encouragement and support of the Irish public. This popular support was and continues to be a very significant influence on the high level of public support for Ireland's overseas aid programme.

I

What it means to be a Lay Missionary

In an article entitled *What it Means to be a Lay Missionary* published in the IMU Report in 2012, Viatores Christi volunteer of twenty five years (most of it with the Sisters of Charity of the Incarnate Word) Miriam Bannon outlined what the lay missionary impulse meant for her.

This is how she described it: "My faith has everything to do with my identity as a missionary. I have faith in a church of communion and participation, inclusive and missionary; a church which identifies with the poor and marginalised and which promotes justice; a church which announces, inaugurates and sows seeds of the Kingdom.

"So what's the difference between a lay missionary, a peace corps volunteer and a development worker when we are united in a similar vision of building communities and their individual members? The answer does not reside in my doing explicitly religious work (catechesis, liturgy, etc.). I am involved in the same day to day work as any other NGO or government development worker. We both work towards ending gender, racial, and ethnic discrimination. We are in solidarity with migrants regardless of their immigration status. We work on the margins towards forming an alternative economic system based on dignified work and living conditions for everybody. We build peace through conflict prevention, conflict management, and post-conflict reconciliation. We support the development of just institutions at all levels of society.

"The difference for me lies in motivation. Anchored in faith, my work is an intentional expression of mission, a striving for the reign of God."

"Over and over again I have been asked why I haven't become a sister. This holds an implicit presupposition: the only way to do long term, lifetime and sustainable missionary work is by joining a religious community in its present form. The term 'laity' is derived from the Greek 'laos' meaning 'a people, a tribe, or a population gathering'. So I, as a lay missionary, am called to serve the people, to be in solidarity with the poor."

The 2013 annual report of Viatores Christi mentioned the positive change that Miriam brought about in her volunteering in community development that year. This included: "parish leaders reported change in themselves – great confidence in their ability to empathise and communicate, thus strengthening their capacity to reach out and be of service to the wider community and a resultant positive response from the community."

Lay missionary volunteers empower those around them, and can bring about social change that is inspired by their faith values. They understand the importance of not just natural, physical, and financial capital, but equally human capital consisting of people's health, knowledge, skills and motivation. They also understand social capital which is concerned with the institutions that help us to maintain and develop human capital in partnership with others such as families, communities, businesses, trade unions, schools and voluntary organisations.

'Harambee' is a Swahili word which means 'working together'. That's what lay mission volunteering is all about.

11
The Role of Lay Missionaries – overseas and at home
Jane Mellett

For many years in Ireland, the word missionary conjured up images of missionary sisters and priests working in Africa, Asia and South America. Iconic missionary congregations like the Medical Missionaries of Mary, Kiltegan Fathers, Columban Fathers and Columban Sisters, Mercy Sisters, Holy Rosary Sisters, Spiritans and many more were household names. With the decline in numbers of vocations to religious life, the landscape has changed quite dramatically and the connection

Missionary volunteer, Jane Mellett, sharing music with a group of Indian youths   *Courtesy Jane Mellet*

147

between your average parish and 'mission' overseas is becoming more fragmented.

At the *Mission Today and Tomorrow Conference*, the role of lay missionaries (LMs) today was explored. Many delegates acknowledged the positive contribution that LMs have made to mission and development worldwide and how they are an integral part of the Irish missionary story. Although two of the original lay missionary groups, Viatores Christi and Volunteer Missionary Movement, have been in existence for the past fifty years, the lay missionary movement in Ireland has grown rapidly in the last ten years. Most religious congregations now offer opportunities for people to experience living and working overseas with their international communities. These experiences vary from two-week immersion programmes to skills-based roles of up to two years or more.

While it is widely recognised the positive contribution that Irish LMs have made to overseas development and to mission there are also challenges which must be addressed. For example, it is essential that sending organisations create responsible programmes which include adequate pre-departure training and support as well as ongoing formation for the duration of the placement and on return. Most missionary organisations have acknowledged the importance of such formation and many, but not all, are members and signatories to *Comhlamh's Code of Good Practice* for overseas volunteering. They have clear objectives and policies in place which aim to ensure that the experience is a beneficial one for all – the host community,

Young Indian boys are keen to learn to read with help from missionary volunteer, Christy Hicks   *Jane Mellet*

the volunteer and the sending organisation. This is an important development for the lay missionary movement as all sending organisations must address the debates surrounding overseas volunteering where many will ask the question: Whom does this benefit?

The reality for many communities in developing countries is that there are key roles for LMs who can mentor local religious and local trainers. Congregations can focus on identifying significant areas that need attention on the ground and they can seek LMs who can offer their abilities, especially during these transition times for many religious congregations in mission countries and in specialised sectors – for example, training for special needs teachers; child safeguarding procedures, or self-assessment tools.

For many organisations today, LMs are recruited to specific placements that will strengthen local partner capacity, allowing them to be more effective in tackling poverty. There is no doubt that the LM experience has the potential to contribute to a new awareness or understanding about a particular justice issue and culture. It allows people to enhance their understanding of the world around them in order to improve it. This should be an integral part of any responsible volunteer programme or mission experience.

While the opportunities for placement are many, the question remains surrounding the homeward journey. Thousands of LMs have travelled from Ireland to work in developing countries, and in doing so have forged strong links with the religious congregations involved in those placements. While many congregations are committed to pre-departure training and journey with individuals while on placement, there are many lost opportunities once a LM returns to Ireland.

LM organisations have a responsibility to their volunteers on return to ensure that their role is nourished, supported and directed in some way. If this happens, the LM becomes a huge asset to the mission experience, the congregation and potentially the Irish Church. It can be extremely difficult to 're-adjust' to life in Ireland and to process the overseas experience. The challenge for all is how to channel the LM experience through reflection and into action. The Irish Church does not know how to embrace returned LMs, and that is a missed opportunity for all involved.

The LM, having lived and worked alongside a religious community structure abroad, will (hopefully) have had an experience of journeying with that faith community on many levels, seeing Gospel values in action, praying and working together towards a vision of a better world. There is a deep faith development experience involved for the LM. Is this then completely lost on the return journey? Where do they go to find that sense of community and passion for justice and peace issues in the local Irish church? Is any of this being captured on the return journey? How many of our lay missionaries are being encouraged and guided into action on return, preaching in parishes, leading workshops, retreats and development education at all levels? One key area to explore is parish twinning. It is through such initiatives that the local church in Ireland can rediscover its purpose in building a community of mission, communion and relationships.

As the face of the Irish missionary may no longer be present throughout Ireland, the LM has the potential to promote support for aid, in being the link, the face of a project advocating support in Ireland for local partnerships. They can serve as important reservoirs of knowledge which will strengthen development programmes and support international solidarity. The energy and enthusiasm of a returned LM can play a major role in development education in Ireland, helping others to explore the root causes of poverty and calling on civil and religious organisations to act. We should not take for granted the links forged between Ireland and developing countries through Irish missionaries. Can we keep this flame alive?

The Lay Missionary Union of Ireland (LMUI) was founded in 2015 as a response to the needs addressed at the *Mission Today and Tomorrow Conference*, and a commitment by 18 LM groups in Ireland to continue to develop a missionary movement in, and from, Ireland into the future. LMUI is a union of missionaries and faith-inspired volunteers, sending and receiving lay groups, acting in solidarity to meet common objectives and needs. Currently sponsored by the Irish Missionary Union, its main objectives are to establish a gathering place for lay missionaries and also to organise regional support to explore and address the needs of those who have returned. Another key objective is to raise awareness of the potential role of returned lay missionaries within the Irish Church and to lobby within the Church to develop funding and support structures for long term Irish LMs.

Jim Farrell, co-ordinator of LMUI notes: "One of the key pieces of work which needs to be done in the Irish Church is to promote the awareness of lay missionaries and volunteers at all levels when they are working abroad and also when they return to Ireland where they can bring expertise into their parishes, dioceses, schools and workplaces." He states that this is where LMUI can do something truly wonderful and far-reaching in the Irish Church working with dioceses across Ireland: "Imagine having small 'hubs' of returned missionaries (lay and religious) working together in dioceses/parishes across Ireland giving a boost to existing initiatives in pastoral work, providing pastoral training for lay leadership initiatives, establishing justice and peace groups and much more. Imagine a renewed Church in Ireland which connects with people and which is prophetic in its work, speaking to issues of the day."

We know that mission is changing, that Ireland is now mission territory also. LMs have a role to play here calling out to all that the Kingdom of God is not just a nice story we hear about on a Sunday; we are meant to be active in eradicating poverty in all its forms across the world; promoting peace and justice and caring for our common home. Then perhaps, through that witness of the Gospel, life will be poured back into our local church.

Good development work and mission need: "alliances, contracts, counterparts, compacts, fellowship, sisterhood, solidarity and straight forward, honest to goodness international co-operation across the board" (A. Fowler. *The Quality of Aid and Development Partnerships, Focus*, Winter 2000, p.11). It is for those charged with the task ahead to say what they need from Irish missionaries in the immediate future. The role of the lay missionary can potentially play an integral part in this. Collaboration between lay, religious, north, south, east, and west will be key for the legacy of Irish mission and development into the future. As the aboriginal woman's response to mission workers quoted in *Ehrics (2000) Volunteering in Development: A Post-Modernist View* says: "If you've come to help me, you're wasting your time… But if you've come because your liberation is bound with mine, then let us go together."

Jane Mellett is a parish pastoral worker in the Archdiocese of Dublin. She is a returned lay missionary having spent several placements with the Salesians in Karnataka, India through SAVIO (Salesian Volunteers Ireland and Overseas).

III

Local and Indigenous Missionaries encourage Lay Mission

Sierra Leonean-born, Sr. Clare Stanley, Assistant Superior General of the Sisters of St. Joseph of Cluny, pointed to the need for lay missionaries when she addressed the *Mission Today & Tomorrow Conference*:

"Mission was linked too much with priests and religious in the past. It was their duty," she said. "The lack of vocations in the west has forced us to rethink this. We would be fools not to draw a lesson from this western experience, and open up formation for mission to lay people today. Evangelisation is the mission of all Christians. It is not reserved for priests, brothers and sisters. Today in Africa, we always have to be vigilant about putting the wrong person in a job just because he is a priest or brother or she is a sister."

She continued: "Here, I want to make a strong appeal for help in the training of local leaders. We need leaders who can help us in the reflection, not only on our role in responding to major challenges such as poverty, corruption, drug trafficking, the trafficking of women and children and so forth, but also in reflecting on the link between our beliefs and our progress."

"Leadership is about leading in the way of transformation. It is about providing vision and direction. It is about making sure that things get done. It is about taking responsibility. Leadership is not just about adhering to rules. It is not about pomp and ceremony. It is not about clinging to tradition with its emphasis on titles, formality, and hierarchy. Tradition is not meant to lock us in. It offers us a base as we open up to new possibilities," she concluded.

Speaking at the same conference, Sr. Pereka Nyirenda, a Religious Sister of Charity in Zambia, advocated collaboration with lay people. "In situations where we do not have the religious to take over, we need to be open to handing over to a lay person instead. Having said this, I feel we need to trust the laity more and hand over the running of institutions/projects to them, not just because we do not have religious to hand over to, but because it is the best way forward for us – to work in collaboration with the laity," she said.

Missionary volunteer, Eilis McDonald, working with teachers in the Hope Academy Primary School, Kaihura, Kyenjojo, Uganda delivering a positive discipline programme. She is long serving in Uganda, Kenya and Malawi in the area of teacher training   *Volunteer Missionary Movement*

Chapter Twelve

Parish Twinning:
A New Bridge between Ireland and the Global South

For many decades our missionaries have been a human bridge between Ireland and the Global South. In their letters to families and friends, during their visits home, and through religious magazines they created an understanding of the terrible conditions of poverty, disease, famine, and inequality in developing countries. As illustrated in earlier chapters, the knowledge shared by missionaries influences public and political opinion about development aid. It is now becoming a less familiar experience to hear missionaries on promotion work speak to audiences at Sunday Masses.

As the number of Irish missionaries in the Global South declines further, the traditional human bridge to developing countries will be weakened. However, as some parishes throughout Ireland have discovered, twinning between parishes has created a new bridge and a meaningful link to the Global South.

Through parish twinning, a mutual respect, sharing and understanding is discovered and developed. Through seeing and touching poverty, inequality and marginalisation, parishes in Ireland experience not only the physical needs, but also the humility, dignity, joy, faith, patience and love of the people and a new awareness of the reach of the Catholic Church and its mission throughout the world. Beyond differences of language, race, ethnicity, culture and nation, the twinning of parishes discovers that we are one human family.

These personal relationships based on faith and solidarity are perhaps the most rewarding and most enriching contribution that parish twinning can make. It is collaboration; a partnership based on equality and dignity. It is not paternalistic; it is about empowerment, and the sharing of resources and people in ways which benefit everybody.

Twinning is helpful to the missionary activity of the Catholic Church. It is about creating links to help twinned parishes meet their religious, educational, health and economic needs, and to help them reach their own potential. It encourages solidarity with the people of developing countries in their struggle for democracy, justice and peace, and forms Christian bonds of love and support. It helps twinned parishes to build their own faith communities based on the peace and justice of the gospel.

Twinning promotes mutual enrichment, awareness of other cultures, education and enthusiasm about mission. People become more enthused when they know where their gifts are going and for what specific projects. Within the twinned parishes, school can twin with school, apostolic group with apostolic group, SVP group with SVP group and so on.

In 1997, the US Catholic Conference of Bishops declared: "One special way parishes have reached out in solidarity is through a process known as twinning … We welcome twinning relationships and encourage the development of these relationships in ways that avoid dependency and paternalism. These bridges of faith offer as much to US parishes as their partners. We are evangelised and changed as we help other communities of faith."

The practice of town twinning has been well established in Ireland, firstly, under the auspices of the United Towns Organisations, and from 2004 under the umbrella of the World Organisation of United Cities. In a town twinning guide that I produced for Junior Chamber Ireland in 1979, then Taoiseach (prime minister), Jack Lynch wrote: "Town twinning, which unites two or more towns in a spirit of equality and reciprocity, is an instrument of human culture and international civic training sustained by practical exchanges of people, ideas and services … it gives international relations a human dimension and each citizen becomes an active ambassador of their country."

Twinning at parish and school levels has garnered some interest too. In an article in the *IMU Report* of May/July 1999, Fr. Tom Kiggins SPS wrote: "The partnership idea is worthy of study and consideration by missionary interests. As Irish missionaries decrease in number, we can no longer take for granted the ready-made links between Ireland and the missionary world which their presence in large numbers ensured."

He continued: "The missionary is a bridge between the community of origin and the community of mission. It is widely accepted that these links are of benefit to both sides in terms of understanding, acceptance and financial assistance. Promotion and mission awareness work in parishes was built on these personal links and continues to benefit from them. As they begin to grow more tenuous, it would be worthwhile for missionaries to explore the partnership and exchange concept as something that might encourage Irish people to continue to take an interest in those churches which received the faith through Irish missionaries and their supporters at home. Such an interest would in turn ensure openness to mission in the future."

Concluding, he encouraged missionaries to: "Look to the future and give some consideration to the idea of community partnerships or twinning as a means of keeping the flame of mission alive in Ireland." The websites of the Irish Redemptorists and St. Patrick's Missionary Society encourage twinning.

In 1999, the Vatican's *Congregation for the Evangelisation of Peoples* issued an instruction on mission co-operation in which it recognised twinning as a valid form of direct co-operation between churches. In 2009 the IMU published *A Guide for Parish Twinning Relationships* which contains a lot of practical advice.

The Irish Aid funded *WorldWise Global Schools Programme* is a 'one-stop-shop' for post primary schools that want to engage in development education. It offers a range of supports to embed development education into teaching and learning, including through global school partnerships. It offers excellent guidance on starting, developing and sustaining a partnership including the drafting of a partnership agreement to provide clarity on expectations and actions. It also provides limited funding.

The Westport – Aror Partnership

The longest-established parish twinning or partnership in Ireland is between Westport in the Archdiocese of Tuam and Aror in the Diocese of Eldoret in the Rift Valley region of Kenya. The Westport-Aror Partnership was founded in 1982 by a few local people led by the vision of businessman, Michael O'Donnell.

Careful planning went into the project which was inspired by a television programme on the pre-existing partnership between Waterford and Kitui in Kenya. The Westport group contacted the IMU where they were given a model to work from, and a choice of the Philippines, Kenya or Mauritius. They knew they had to make sure that there was an Irish presence in the country, that language wouldn't be a significant barrier, that accessibility to the region was practical, and that the government of the country that they decided on was amenable to external help.

The remote Aror region with 18,000 inhabitants in the Keiro Valley in north western Kenya fitted these prudent criteria and was chosen as a partner. This was the birth of the partnership that has become one of the most enduring and successful in Ireland. Its main aim is to provide vital health services to the people of Aror, saving lives and preventing disease. The Medical Missionaries of Mary, founded in Nigeria but headquartered in Ireland since shortly after their formation, had established a small health clinic in Aror and this became the pivot of the partnership. The nearest hospital is 3-hour drive away on rough roads.

The partnership funds the employment of qualified staff and the purchase of medicines and medical equipment, plus an ambulance that is suitable for the rough terrain. The clinic has been transformed into a modern medical facility with 24 beds. It now provides a wide range of essential medical services including a labour ward. It is estimated that about 4,000 lives have been saved since the partnership was set up, and the health of the community has improved considerably.

Since its establishment 34 years ago, members of the partnership have traveled at their own expense from Westport to Aror every few years to monitor progress and maintain relationships. The Westport committee is clear that missionaries are central to the work of the partnership. In 2000, the Medical Missionaries of Mary handed over the clinic in Aror to the Sisters of St. Joseph of Tarbes. That congregation has no connection with Ireland but the partnership has endured.

That transition from an Irish missionary congregation to a non-Irish/local congregation is a good example of succession in mission. The Westport committee has placed its confidence in the Sisters of St. Joseph of Tarbes as the trustworthy stewards of the funding provided by the partnership.

The partnership continues to raise awareness of the developing world within the local community in Westport which is consistently one of the largest donor parishes to mission collections within the Archdiocese of Tuam – testimony to the words of Fr. Tom Kiggins SPS on "openness to mission." Sr. Siobhán Corkery, Congregational Leader of the Medical Missionaries of Mary says: "The concern, friendship, prayers as well as the financial support are hugely important to those on the ground. It was particularly important in earlier years when communication was not so easy. When someone else cares about what you give your life for, it is both encouraging and empowering."

II
Episcopal Support for Twinning

The Westport – Aror Partnership is strongly supported by the Archbishop of Tuam, Dr. Michael Neary, and by Bishop Cornelius Korir of the Diocese of Eldoret. They concelebrated Mass in St. Mary's Church in Westport to mark its 25th anniversary in November 2007 and again to mark its 30th anniversary in November 2012. In his homilies, Dr. Neary focused on some key elements of successful partnership at parish level. The following are summarised extracts from his homilies on these occasions:

"It is one thing to be committed to eradicating poverty on a global map. However, this experience of partnership has focused minds in a very special way by putting a human face on poverty and helping the development of the Aror area. Schools in the Westport area, primary and post-primary, were introduced to this concept from the very beginning. This was an inspired move and has contributed to the ongoing success of the project.

"In mission, attention must always be given to solidarity. This involves support with our prayers and financially. As Christians, we are a people who are sent to others. There is a never-ending need for mission – for sending. The people of

Westport have reached out in a spirit of love to the people of Aror and have drawn them into communion. In return, they have benefited enormously from their sharing. Partnership involves sensitivity and reverence where joy is at the heart. The message of our sending and being sent is life and joy.

"The clinic in Aror provides vital health services for people of that area. The financial support from Westport provides funding for qualified staff and the purchase of medical equipment and supplies. It is estimated that €700,000 has been donated in humanitarian programmes over the past thirty years, and current fundraising will fund a new ambulance. As a result of this solidarity and love, human suffering has been lessened and pain has been alleviated. It is estimated that the clinic has saved in the region of 4,000 lives during those 30 years. Generous financial support has been instrumental in so many ways.

"Local people in Aror are encouraged to become involved in managing the centre. They are enabled to help themselves. What was initiated and managed by the Medical Missionaries of Mary is now managed by locals in Kenya.

"The people of Westport have benefited too in many ways from this partnership. Awareness of the developing world has been created. Thank God for the people of Aror who have taught us so many lessons. Without this partnership I am convinced that we at home would be all the poorer, inclined to focus on ourselves and refuse to look to and address situations of need. This partnership has contributed to greater social awareness which in our culture today is very welcome.

"We thank God too for the people of vision who originated this partnership. It is a good example to encourage and to motivate other parishes to reach out to other developing communities. It is a rich insight for similar action in partnership."

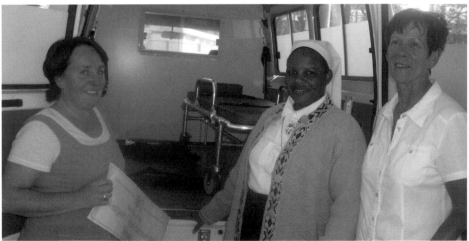

Margaret Joyce and Gertie Foley from Westport handing over a new ambulance to Sr. Mary Mwangi, St. Joseph of Tarbes Sisters in Aror   *Westport – Aror Partnership*

III
Athenry – Simanjiro Partnership

The Divine Word Missionaries (SVD) have a mission in Simanjiro – a small settlement 104km south of Arusha in Tanzania – with three churches and seventeen outstations. The parish is staffed by missionaries from India, but the SVDs have a strong presence in Ireland. Athenry and Simanjiro came into contact, principally, as a consequence of the unexpected death of a local man, Michael Ryan, whose colleagues in Teagasc Athenry decided to do something meaningful in his memory, such as a project in Africa.

Contact was made with Eamonn Brehony – a development consultant living in Arusha, Tanzania – who was doing work for the Simanjiro Animal Husbandry & Vocational Training Centre. He suggested the parish of Simanjiro as a suitable location for support. The Athenry – Simanjiro Partnership was established in 2005 with Nuala King, who had spent a short time teaching in Tanzania, as chairperson. Fr. Tony King, the then parish priest of Athenry, was very supportive of the partnership.

The area of Simanjiro is very remote; there is no electricity, roads are dirt-tracks, with a radio service for the flying medical services operated by the Divine Word Missionaries for emergency transport to hospital. The people who are subsistence farmers are from the Maasai tribe who are pastoral and nomadic. They live in mud huts, drawing water for miles, and eking out a frugal living for their children is a daily challenge.

One of the first projects of the partnership was support through Gorta to the Animal Husbandry & Vocational Training Centre. This was followed by the drilling of a bore hole to supply clean water to the community, small hospital and schools. The parish church was dilapidated and this was replaced by a new one that was inaugurated on 19 October 2008.

Fr. Peter Pinto SVD, the current parish priest in Simanjiro speaks with appreciation about how, through the initiative of the partnership, a number of medical and nursing students and other medical personnel from NUI Galway volunteered and with their fundraising supplied the health centre at Simanjiro with equipment and a new ambulance for the hospital. "A large container brought a big amount of hospital supplies, school supplies and church supplies which were so badly needed," he recalled.

"The partnership supported the local volunteers in Simanjiro who are generally known as catechists by providing them with bicycles, and roofing three village chapels which are being used as church on Sundays and other days of the week as a nursery school. In 2009, the partnership supported the extension of the hospital wards. The existing health centre was just 16 beds and with this expansion, we now can accommodate 50 beds with proper ventilation. There are plans to build a nursery school in the village of Lenjani and to drill a bore well and install a water pump at the headquarters of the Simanjiro District – Orkesment." He continued: "The partnership also made it possible for Fr. Eusebio Manangbao SVD, who was parish priest at Simanjiro, and me to visit Athenry and meet the people and visit schools to express deep gratitude on behalf of the people of Simanjiro for the Christian solidarity of the people of the Athenry area."

The partnership has recently completed the building and fitting out of a new children's home in Nairobi for 24 street children. Again, this was in conjunction with the Asian SVD Province – Fr. Eusebio Manangbao, former parish priest of Simanjiro, being the direct contact.

An interesting aspect of this partnership is that the missionary connection in Simanjiro was Indian rather than Irish. But, like Westport, the missionary presence there was central in its choice as a partner by the Athenry group.

Nuala King says: "The partnership is project specific. All funds are raised for specific projects and none is used for administration. These are important concepts for the partnership – understood clearly on both sides."

Fr. Liam Dunne, Secretary of the British and Irish SVD Province, reporting on a visit to Simanjiro in January 2016, told readers of their magazine: "I was impressed by the nice church and school which were provided by the people of Athenry parish. I also saw the medical equipment which was provided by students from NUI Galway who have an ongoing relationship with the parish and the surrounding area."

Good Shepherd Church in Simanjiro built with funding from the Athenry – Simanjiro Partnership

Athenry – Simanjiro Partnership

IV

Diocese of Meath Schools Twinning Programme

In late October 1998, Hurricane Mitch struck Central America, leaving more than 11,000 people dead, destroying hundreds of thousands of homes and causing more than $5 billion in damage. It was the deadliest hurricane to hit the western hemisphere in more than 200 years. Bishop Michael Smith explains the connection between the natural disaster and the schools twinning programme.

"For almost twenty years it has been the practice of this diocese to send monies donated following major natural disasters directly to the Church in that country. On 29 October 1998 Honduras, and especially its capital, Tegucigalpa, was devastated by Hurricane Mitch. There was a very generous response from the people of the diocese to that disaster and the money received was sent directly to Cardinal Rodriguez Maradiga, Archbishop of Tegucigalpa. For some years afterwards, the diocese continued to support his work of rebuilding the homes of many. He rebuilt a township to house people who lost everything in the floods, naming one of its streets Mullingar Street in recognition of the help he received from the Diocese of Meath."

"Previous to that, the diocese had links with Zambia through Mercy Sisters from Co. Meath who are still working there, and with Uganda through Mill Hill Missionaries from these parts too. As I knew the Nuncio for Thailand and Myanmar, based in Bangkok, the links with the Church there developed from the tsunami disaster of 26 December 2004. He had been in the Nunciature in Dublin for a number of years and developed links with many priests in this diocese. Irish priests, sisters, brothers and lay volunteers had worked in all the countries affected by the tsunami. As the full horror of the loss of life and devastation caused by the tsunami unfolded, it was obvious that major help was needed. I asked the priests to offer an opportunity to the faithful in the diocese to contribute to the relief effort. The response in this diocese, as in all parts of the country, was extraordinarily generous with over €1.1 million being donated by 69 parishes."

"In my statement to parishes about the distribution of this money to the churches in the affected countries, I said that it was my hope that the diocese could continue to support the rebuilding efforts in South East Asia over the coming years. One possible option was that schools in this diocese may be able to 'adopt' schools in affected regions with a view to providing ongoing support and dialogue. In doing so, we would have done 'no more than our duty' before the Lord."

"The Columbans, through their base in this diocese, were an obvious link with Myanmar where they ministered in two dioceses in the north east bordering China.

They had established a number of schools in the area. These were very basic, but still operating. They needed major updating, and the diocese agreed with the Columbans to co-fund this work. The twinning with the schools catering for the children of Myanmar refugees on the Thai border grew out of this. It operates through the National Catholic Commission for Migrants. In all, 13 primary schools are involved with 10 schools in very remote areas in Thailand-Myanmar where access is very difficult."

"The links continue with support also being extended to Cardinal Bo in Yangon. The solidarity and the sharing of information and culture have been good for the children involved, and one would like to expand it. I feel that involvement of schools in this part of the world with those in poorer areas is good for all involved, not least the children in these parts. It is an antidote to the self-interest and selfishness that animates so much in society in these times."

"There is also a number of schools – mostly with Mercy links – supporting the Mercy Sisters in Zambia with fund-raising events. A number of boys' post-primary schools, including two diocesan colleges, send out a group of students every few years in a volunteering programme. This was started by the Christian Brothers linking up with Brothers' schools in Zambia and in India," concluded Bishop Smith.

Apart from refurbishing ramshackle schools, most of which have no running water or electricity, children in Meath diocese write to their friends on the other side of the world sharing stories from their lives and learning from each other. The sixth class children donate part of their confirmation gifts to support the schools for the Burmese migrant children. This enables the children to have books, pencils and lunches on their school days.

Bishop Smith visited Myanmar in 2009 and afterwards it was decided to assist with an educational project for young people in the Diocese of Banmaw which is located in the north of Myanmar. It has 18 boarding houses for students, often from remote parts of the region, who are helped to attend state schools, given accommodation, food and additional tuition. Like with the missionaries, education is seen as the foundation to lift these students out of the cycle of poverty.

Brigid Weir, co-ordinator of the diocesan twinning programme has visited Myanmar and Thailand to monitor and report on progress. When she met the Finance Officer of the UN High Commission for Refugees in Myanmar, he spoke with great praise for the work that the Catholic Church was doing to provide basic needs and education for the refugees. In fact, he said, most of the support and concern for the refugees was provided by the Catholic Church. Of course, this is a pattern of solidarity that is the norm in most developing countries.

V

School Twinning

Queen of the Rosary School in Bo in Sierra Leone, under the auspices of the Missionary Sisters of the Holy Rosary, is twinned with St. Mary's Christian Brothers School in Enniscorthy in Ireland. This link was established in the 2007/2008 academic year for inter-cultural exchange and enrichment between both schools.

Sr. Bernadine Ngozi MSHR speaks about the enhancement of shared learning experiences between students and teachers of both schools. "This has been accompanied by several exchange visits by some teachers and students of each school. During these visits we participate in the teaching and learning processes of the other school. We enter their classrooms, take lessons, share about our educational system, participate in the school's annual sports meeting, discuss our school's unique challenges and together seek possible ways of improving on them. For instance, we decided together two years ago to embark on a common project of health and safety in each school. This was successful. With Sierra Leone experiencing the Ebola outbreak in 2014, together we explored possible ways of enhancing personal hygiene in our own little ways. This exchange has been working pretty well," she said.

VI

Church Mission Society of the Anglican Church

Twinning is an activity of the Anglican Church too. In April 2006, the Church of Ireland Templebreedy group of parishes launched a school twinning project between their parish school in Crosshaven, Co. Cork and St Michael's School for the Blind in Ranchi, Northern India.

The Rector, Rev. Isobel Jackson, who with her family volunteered in East Africa for a number of years as mission partners, says: "This link is part of development education and commitment of our school and parish to raising our sense of global consciousness and partnership between us and the Global South."

"Our partnership is precisely that: a two-way relationship between our two schools and parish where we both have the opportunity to give and to receive. Following a visit by two staff and two pupils to India in April 2006, we were thrilled to welcome two staff and two pupils back to Ireland in March 2008. The human contact has brought our project to life for the children in both schools," she said.

The Church Mission Society of the Anglican Church established a presence in Ireland in 1814. One of its objectives is to establish partnership links for its churches here with those within its global partners' network. Currently, it has nineteen such links in nine countries in Africa and Nepal. Another one of these is the Parish of Christ Church, Delgany, Co. Wicklow and the Anglican Diocese of Yei, in South Sudan. Its philosophy is that "mission is at its best when it's personal – when people engage with people and share their lives with one another."

VII
Other Types of Twinning Partnerships

Young Social Innovators (YSI) was founded in Ireland in 2001 by Sr. Stanislaus Kennedy RSC. What started as a small project is now a national programme with over 70,000 young people involved in what is the largest social innovation programme for young people in Ireland, allowing them to become active social citizens in their communities.

A large crowd gather for the opening of the Good Shepherd Church in Simanjiro in 2008
Athenry – Simanjiro Partnership

In 2014, the YSI Programme extended its work to Canada and South Korea, and in 2015 it was extended to Zambia. The extension to Zambia followed an interest expressed by some Zambian teachers from the Kaoma district in the Western Province of Zambia, whose school is linked to a YSI school in Ireland. This was initiated by the Presentation Sisters. Their students have collaborated together on projects over the years. When teachers visited and saw YSI events and learning first hand, they asked if YSI Ireland could train teachers to engage more schools in Zambia. Thus, the ball was set rolling.

The invitation was then extended to Religious Sisters of Charity schools, and through the work of Sr. Pereka Nyirenda RSC who served for twelve years on her congregation's leadership team in Dublin, secondary schools in Lusaka were identified and invited to participate in a pilot programme which began in January 2016 with eight schools. The aim is that the programme will take root in Zambia and thus contribute to building up a population of active and responsible citizens among the youth of the country. Again, what was a small seed in the Presentation School partnership has sparked a programme of social innovation that has huge potential for the youth of Zambia. The Zambian Department of Education has expressed interest in the programme.

The St. Vincent de Paul Society (SVP) General Council officially launched twinning in 1954, and has twinning officers at regional levels. The aims of the programme are to facilitate communication between conferences around the world, promoting a spirit of understanding, friendship and solidarity among all Vincentians, and to alleviate misery and hunger. It also aims to promote social justice throughout the world, to animate solidarity within the Society worldwide, to be a witness of Christian charity, and to promote the establishment of new councils and conferences by helping them to start and expand. The Society in Ireland is currently linked with eleven English speaking countries in sub-Saharan Africa.

The Irish League of Credit Unions Foundation has twinning arrangements across various sectors such as teaching and electricity supply in developing countries. Activities carried out are defined on the basis of local needs and are aimed at strengthening the technical and financial operation of credit unions. For example, the INTO Credit Union has a twenty-year relationship with the Gambia Teachers Union Co-Operative Credit Union that has a membership of 22,000. Michael McHugh, CEO of the INTO Credit Union points out that this partnership is an empowerment model in an evolving financial sub-sector. The Gambia Ireland Volunteers in Education, founded in 1974, also operates a teacher volunteering programme in The Gambia.

At country level, the Sierra Leone Ireland Partnership was set up in 1991 to advocate for the needs of Sierra Leone where the first Irish missionaries arrived in the 1860s. Sr. Dr. Hilary Lyons MSHR has served as president of the partnership since 2000. Ireland opened a diplomatic and development aid mission in Sierra Leone in 2005, and it became a partner country in the Irish Aid programme in 2013. A full embassy was opened in Freetown in 2014.

VIII
Twinning Partnerships are about Solidarity

The focus of the five examples of twinning partnerships detailed in this chapter is chiefly on health and education which is in line with the traditional activities of Irish missionaries, and the WHO's Global School Health Initiative. That initiative, launched in 1995, seeks to mobilise and strengthen health promotion and education activities at the local, national, regional and global levels. The Initiative is designed to improve the health of students, school personnel, families and other members of the community through schools.

However, the total influence and impact of these partnerships is much wider in terms of solidarity, global consciousness, humanitarian and development aid, culture, values and social justice based on equality and the spirit of the gospels. Each of them is different, but they share the same Christian values seeing the global church as one body – our brothers and sisters in Christ.

These partnerships are an inspiration and an encouragement to parishes throughout Ireland to consider twinning as a bridge to a parish in the Global South, thereby facilitating engagement in missionary outreach following in the footsteps of thousands of Irish missionaries.

Brigid Weir, Twinning Co-Ordinator for Diocese of Meath meeting Brendan Rogers, Irish Ambassador in Thailand and Myanmar in 2016   *Courtesy Brigid Weir*

Chapter Thirteen

Missionary Development is Integral to Ireland's Aid Programme

In Chapter 5 we saw the influence of Irish missionaries on the evolution of Ireland's overseas aid programme in the early 1970s. Since then, for well grounded policy and practical reasons, the Irish government has supported the development work of missionaries in the Global South. This was done through APSO and its embassies up until 2004 when IMRS (now Misean Cara) was set up as a dedicated agency to distribute public funds for missionary development projects.

In 2006, the White Paper on Irish Aid set out some of those reasons when it stated: "Irish missionary organisations have been pioneers in the area of development cooperation. Their work predates that of the government's development programme and, in some respects, we have followed their lead… Missionary organisations have built up considerable expertise and have extensive networks through which they can deliver assistance. The role and work of missionaries also continues to have a strong resonance with the Irish people and enjoys considerable support."

Ronan Murphy, retired Director General of Irish Aid, in his book *Inside Irish Aid: the Impulse to Help* (The Liffey Press, 2012, page 11) explains the empathy of the Irish people with the Global South and concludes: "There is no one explanation. But the overwhelming view of those I interviewed for this book was that it is, above all, the missionaries we have to thank for the interest which Ireland takes in the developing world. I saw that Ireland had a huge advantage when it started out in that the missionary tradition had built up a real connection, especially with Africa, which resonated with the Irish public. None of the new EU member states had such strong connections."

Chapter 6 in this publication illustrates the current strategies of the German and British governments for collaboration with religious actors in pursuit of their aid programmes.

Referring to the low risk associated with missionaries, Murphy said: "Whilst some of the programmes Irish Aid spent money on kept me awake at night, the funding that went through missionaries never did." Giving increased support to the missionaries out of the growing budget was a popular decision with politicians and the Irish public because of the empathy they enjoyed. The Irish government always strives for cross-party support in the Oireachtas (parliament) and for the public's support for its overseas aid programme. That is prudent, as the programme is central to Ireland's foreign policy.

Throughout this book, mention is made of the networks available to missionaries and FBOs. A fine example of those networks and outreach was that of the late Sr. Dr. Maura O'Donoghue, a member of the Medical Missionaries of Mary and a medical doctor. From 1987 she led CAFOD's pioneering response to the escalating global HIV/AIDS pandemic. By 1994, CAFOD was not only managing 95 of its own HIV-related projects, but also a further 60 projects on behalf of other Caritas and CIDSE agencies in 36 countries throughout Africa, Asia, Eastern Europe and Latin America. Working closely with Fr. Bob Vitillo at Caritas Internationalis in Rome, Sr. Maura targeted national and regional meetings of bishops' conferences, meetings of religious, Caritas networks, diocesan meetings of priests and religious, seminaries and theological institutes in Africa, Asia and Latin America, to raise their awareness of the reality of HIV and to canvass their support for Church-based responses that became pivotal in the global response to that pandemic.

These unique global networks of missionaries are recognised by the Irish state. President Michael D. Higgins opened *The Face of Mercy Today* photographic exhibition on 25 September 2014 to mark Mercy Day with the Sisters of Mercy in Dublin. In his address he stated: "The partnership with missionaries is of real importance in the achievement of our government's overseas development objectives."

Continuing, he said: "The Sisters of Mercy have been part of a larger global family engaging in missionary work across the world. They have travelled to remote and challenging environments, teaching, administering to the sick, and working

President Higgins being presented with a copy of the 2014 Annual Report of Misean Cara by then Board Chairman, Matt Moran   *Keith Arkins*

relentlessly to relieve poverty and suffering. There, they brought with them so much that is best about our Irish reputation abroad, defining it through their great humanitarian work across the globe. They did so, and continue to do so, with such an assiduousness for justice and equality that has enabled them to ensure lasting change for some of the most marginalised and vulnerable communities in the world. Today, as a global network, the Mercy International Association is critically positioned to ensure that the voices – and most importantly, the fundamental rights – of the most marginalised are heard and advocated for at a global level," he concluded.

Using these networks over the decades, missionaries have delivered efficiently and cost-effectively with the state funding and the donations they receive from their vast army of supporters. In 2013, Irish Aid engaged an independent consultant to review the expenditure of its grant aid to Misean Cara. In his report, he stated: "The programmes and projects implemented by Misean Cara members target the poorer, more vulnerable and marginalised sections of society to a large degree. The overall range of beneficiaries is very high and includes specific targeting of widows, orphans and vulnerable children, child-headed households, low-income families, refugees and internally displaced persons, victims of natural emergencies, wars and crime, minority communities, people living with HIV & AIDS, disabled people, pastoralists, people living in remote rural areas, urban slum-dwellers, illiterate people and prisoners, among others."

The consultant went on to discuss future funding to missionaries thus: "As the

Sally McEllistrim, World Missions Ireland joins Fr. Henry Chiwayah on a visit to the bush in Zomba Diocese, Malawi to offer Sunday Mass
World Missions Ireland

presence of Irish missionaries in the field continues to decline, there is an argument for saying that Misean Cara should now be phased out slowly, as it was founded for the specific purpose of supporting the projects of Irish missionaries. However, given the huge level of commitment that missionaries have shown over decades and even centuries, it would be extremely unsatisfactory from the perspective of the congregations themselves (and from the perspective of the Irish public that has strongly supported them), if there was no long term legacy from that work, and no further connection with Ireland for the congregations on the ground."

"Hence, in the view of the author, the preferred option would be to continue funding of local congregations as partners of the Irish congregations where it is appropriate and realistic to do so. Particular care should be taken to ensure that ownership issues are fully addressed so that the continuing links between Irish congregations and the implementing agencies on the ground are genuine and strong, and that the Irish congregations can fully stand over the work being implemented by their local congregations or partner agencies."

Minister of State Joe Costello emphasised this message when he addressed the *Mission Today & Tomorrow Conference*: "After such a long legacy of quality missionary work, now we have to focus on sustaining it."

1

The Role of Misean Cara within the Irish Missionary Movement

It would be difficult to write about the recent period of the Irish missionary movement, and particularly its future, without referring to Misean Cara and the very significant role it plays in the development activities of that movement. *The Ireland Aid Review* (2002) made specific recommendations regarding grant aid to missionaries. That was in the context of change in aid modalities generally and aid structures within Ireland. In October 2002, consultants reviewing IMU structures for the distribution of Ireland Aid and APSO assistance to missionaries found the need for "a separate agency within IMU to provide for the legal autonomy and capacities required." They also proposed the establishment of a working group involving APSO/Ireland Aid and the IMU to manage the funding and structural changes.

The government closed APSO in January 2004, and in June of that year the Irish Missionary Resource Service Ltd (IMRS) was set up by the IMU. That name was changed to Misean Cara in 2008 – 'cara' being the Irish word for friend. Here we see friendship and solidarity enshrined into the name of a pivotal body within the missionary movement.

As a funding agency, Misean Cara has a unique structure. Being fully-funded by the government, it is not an NGO. It is a membership-based and intermediary organisation comprised of 87 religious congregations and two lay missionary sending organisations. In June 2016, the Church Mission Society of the Anglican Church became a member. Misean Cara is governed by a board of directors who volunteer their time and skills. The closest comparable organisations in Europe are the Swedish Mission Council and the Danish Mission Council which are grant-aided by their respective governments, but one difference is that those countries do not send ordained or vowed missionaries similar to Ireland, they send lay missionary volunteers.

Misean Cara is a faith-inspired organisation as set out in its 2015 vision statement. *The Ireland Aid Review* 2002, when dealing with civil society, separated NGOs and missionaries into different chapters which was welcomed by missionaries to indicate their distinctive role. Significantly, the difference between NGOs and FBOs was recognised in the report on the consultation among donor organisations, UN development agencies and FBOs held in New York on 12-13 May 2014. It stated that 'a FBO is different than other types of partners, even other organisations that are member-driven'. Recognition of that difference, especially by donor agencies, is significant for the reasons outlined in Chapter 6.

During its evolution, and similar to above Councils, Misean Cara has extended its remit to include training and capacity building of its members and their partner organisations in the Global South. It receives an annual grant from Irish Aid – currently €15.5 million Euro – within a legal framework that sets out criteria and benchmarks to be delivered within agreed time scales and reported on in the results framework system. Irish Aid carries out monitoring and evaluation of its activities as well as audit reviews. A company with charitable status, it was an early signatory to The Governance Code for the CVC Sector in Ireland.

Member organisations can apply for grants. Applications go through an approval process with the successful applicants submitting detailed reports on outcomes and results achieved in grant-aided projects. Some of these projects would be best described as programmes with many of them also grant-aided by other donors and supported by local government agencies in many countries.

Misean Cara has been successful in supporting congregations in improving further the quality and effectiveness of their planning, execution, monitoring, evaluation, measurement of impact, financial and risk management, child safeguarding and reporting on the results and the impact of development projects and programmes.

That success is achieved through funding but equally through a range of capacity building activities such as regular general or consultation meetings, special interest group dialogue, workshop discussions, mentoring scheme in Africa, country meetings on various continents, information newsletters, social media communications, and field visits by Misean Cara personnel.

Additionally, the practice of development projects being implemented by a group of congregations has pioneered working in consortia at field level in the south. All of this enriches peer to peer and collaborative learning by missionaries. Collaboration not only in what they do in their works, but also in their relationships – how they think, plan, organise, learn, believe and hope is a true sign of vitality of religious life today.

The range of support activities provided by Misean Cara is significant compared to other donor agencies. This training and capacity building has improved their skills in project planning and implementation, and in dealing with other donors as access to funding generally becomes more competitive. The need for congregations to expand their knowledge of development approaches and evolving issues, and technical skills to strengthen implementation capacity and impact is recognised by many of them who send their members for further education in development related studies and training programmes in various institutes. Misean Cara does not operate a study fellowship awards programme nor provide online skills training or coaching.

Within congregations there is also a growing number of lay employees in development offices who are highly competent in development practices and project management. Their knowledge and skills are regularly shared within working groups for the benefit of all congregations.

As transition to local members continues apace, bespoke training and coaching remains necessary in some developing countries to improve general leadership skills and the strategic visionary competence of young local missionaries who are assuming leadership roles within their congregations and want to create their own momentum. This need was outlined clearly during consultations with missionaries undertaken in Africa and Latin America by Dr. Margaret Nugent of NUI Maynooth in 2007, and it was echoed during the *Mission Today & Tomorrow Conference* in 2013.

We saw in Chapter 12 that *WorldWise Global Schools* (WWGS) is the national programme for development education at post primary level in Ireland and, like Misean Cara, it is funded by Irish Aid. Whilst Misean Cara does not have a specific development education function, its member organisations have been engaged throughout Ireland since the 1920s in what could be described broadly as development education, or certainly as the creation of awareness of the Global South.

The Presentation Sisters and the Jesuits have specific development education programmes operating in their schools in Ireland, whilst the Christian Brothers and other congregations have various immersion programmes for students to experience developing countries. The IMU and World Missions Ireland (WMI) engage in extensive promotion of missionary activity, particularly at parish and school levels. For example, WMI interacts with 1,500 primary schools.

There are no links between Misean Cara and WWGS but opportunities exist, for example, in the area of global school partnerships linked to missionaries who provide a solid foundation for enduring partnerships such as we saw in Chapter 12. The message about development by missionaries must be highlighted to young people through a variety of channels.

Missionaries are humble people who rarely seek the lime-light for their work. But this can be a disadvantage in creating public awareness of the value and impact of that work, as well as the geographical shifts within the movement. To create that awareness, especially about development, requires carefully targeted communications to different audiences. These include media personnel, students at second and third levels, teacher training colleges and specific programmes in universities, including masters and doctoral research programmes, and the Ubuntu Network which promotes that development education be embedded into post-primary initial teacher education.

There are opportunities such as media field trips to the Global South, an annual lecture, an annual media award scheme for feature articles or documentaries, public photographic exhibitions and TV documentaries. Misean Cara could play a pivotal role in such activities to help retain the traditional awareness of the developing world that is ever changing.

Misean Cara's vision, adopted in 2015, and its structure are likely to be appropriate for some years to come, but thereafter different architecture and strategies may be necessary to meet a different operating environment of its members. It is a relatively small donor agency by international standards. It has limited resources for engagement in research and policy analysis, for example, within the evolving faith-inspired development arena where learning is an on-going process. However, there are opportunities for links with universities, research bodies, and particularly the newly established international Partnership on Religion and Sustainable Development initiated by the German government.

Trócaire undertakes significant research and policy dialogue on the development issues of the time, and is part of the CIDSE and Caritas networks. It works closely with many missionaries in the Global South, for example, projects of two congregations are part of its country programme in Kenya. Other Christian FBOs have formed networks such as Act Alliance to increase their global impact, particularly in policy and advocacy, knowing that any one organisation does not have all the answers in the complex arena of development. Misean Cara is a member of Dóchas – the NGO network – but collaboration with Trócaire and other FBOs could broaden its horizons to scale up its influence.

Many NGOs pursue a policy of acting locally but thinking globally by forming networks or coalitions. FBOs are accountable to larger church structures that give them both local and global reach which positions them with an immediate and distinct advantage in global terms. We saw in Chapter 6 how they build networks and alliances to give them the added advantage of opportunities that stem from the growing interface between faith and development, and to allow them to scale up their influence. They do this by shifting their thinking from projects and programmes to agendas and audiences, along the continuum of research to policy to greater action nationally or trans-nationally. More and more, large donor agencies are seeking this type of architecture when looking for effective agents of development.

Catholic Relief Services in the USA describe the benefits of networks thus: "Building external relations and maintaining healthy and productive partnerships enhances the ability of an organisation to achieve its mission by effectively linking with important and influential groups in the broader environment. Effective relationships enable the organisation to leverage resources and to network with like-minded groups to influence the policy and regulatory environment."

In exercising strategic foresight, Misean Cara is likely to have to consider broader

OLA sisters and friends on their way to an internally displaced persons' camp in Abuja to inaugurate the Maria Centre, a skills training and empowerment project set up in response to the influx of people fleeing conflict in north-eastern Nigeria *OLA Sisters*

development architecture and collaborative arrangements and dialogue in the years ahead. New dynamics will call for fresh responses to new challenges and new opportunities in the evolving development arena where the role of faith is increasing, and the strategic influence of international FBO networks on the world stage is growing. Similar to its member congregations, it will have to face its own transition to sustain itself in a new missionary operating environment.

An example of a development agency that transitioned successfully is Gorta – Ireland's first such agency – which was set up in 1965 as a semi-state body for a specific purpose. In 1998, it changed to NGO status, and in July 2014 it merged with Self Help Africa. In 2015, Gorta-Self Help Africa and Concern Worldwide held discussions and agreed to a project co-operation pact with a view to possible further consolidation within the Irish NGO sector.

Missionary activities funded by Irish Aid through Misean Cara have made a highly significant and distinctive contribution to the success and reputation of Ireland's overseas aid programme of which they are an important part. Missionaries have given geographical spread and added unique value to that programme that would not otherwise have been achievable by Irish Aid.

State funding of missionary development has been, and continues to be, a very

Students of Divine Word Missions studying for the priesthood in India meet Fr. Liam Dunne (front centre), of their British and Irish Province, during his visit in 2016   *Divine Word Missionaries*

prudent investment that is popular with the Irish public and politicians. As the number of Irish-born missionaries declines, a new generation is carrying forward their legacy with the same Christian values, determination, trust and passion to support the poor and marginalised irrespective of class or creed. Ireland's overseas aid programme reaps the benefits of such a values-inspired and passionate army of personnel working amongst the poorest and most deprived communities in the Global South, and it gains those benefits at minimum cost to the Irish taxpayers.

II
How Missionary Development is being Carried Forward
Sr. Loice Kashangura FMSA

The Irish Aid policy – *One World, One Future* – acknowledges that international development cannot be realised until those who live under the chains of misery are helped to break free from their sufferings. It is within that context that the place of missionaries as important collaborators in the Irish development aid programme in the past, now and into the future is positioned.

Over the years, Ireland has considered missionaries an essential component of the Irish Aid programme. The Minister of Trade and Development, Joe Costello, acknowledged this in his address to the Misean Cara 2012 Annual General Meeting and reiterated in his address at the *Mission Today and Tomorrow Conference* when he said: "Irish missionaries were the pioneers in the area of development cooperation, predating our own official aid programme. Indeed, you led the way for much of what the government is now doing in the area of development assistance. The influence of the missionaries is reflected in Irish Aid's focus on poverty reduction, on hunger, its commitment to avoiding any form of tied aid and its strong solidarity with those is greatest need."

The missionaries' greatest contribution is their empathy and solidarity with the people they love and work with. We relate this to present realities in the communities where poverty levels are still high, and children go hungry and die of treatable diseases. It is in these needy communities that missionaries continue to render invaluable services to uplift those whose situations cannot permit them to liberate themselves without external help.

The desire for the well-being of all humanity is a mark in the Irish identity such that even in the midst of economic challenges, the above policy on international development expresses a renewed commitment to helping the developing world. It states: "Our history will not allow us to ignore the reality that hunger is a daily fact of life for many people in developing countries today. We do this because of our sense of justice and compassion, born of a history of famine, suppression and conflict. And we do it because it is the right thing to do in an increasingly inter-connected world. ... and the Irish people can be extremely proud of the difference that we make to the lives of millions of families who struggle to survive on less than €1.25 a day."

Indeed, solidarity is an indispensable dimension of authentic development, arising from our common roots as people, the living image of a compassionate God. It calls us to participate in relieving the sufferings of others. As missionaries, we are constantly challenged to act in ways that help bring about positive change in the lives of the marginalised and most vulnerable. Down through the years, the Irish have expressed a strong trust in their missionaries helping the downtrodden in various parts of the world – a trust that is repeated by local communities whom they accompany in their struggles and their joys in Africa and elsewhere.

We commend the 2006 White Paper for acknowledging the Irish aid programme as, "A practical expression of the values that help define what it means to be Irish." (Bertie Ahern, An Taoiseach). Solidarity with the developing countries, therefore, implies that Irish Aid continues to consider missionaries as vital partners in development aid to reduce the level of poverty and inequalities in communities that need help most. Missionaries are well placed because of their faith-inspired commitment to the poor and suffering who may not have access to any external aid apart from that which is channeled through missionaries.

Some of the greatest strengths of missionaries in development work include that they are trustworthy, dependable and effective. A World Bank report in 2000 asserts that faith-based groups are the most trusted institutions precisely because they are both embedded in and committed to local communities. Because missionaries are trusted by the people they serve, they are well placed to collaborate with local communities in a two-way process, facilitating community participation, and promoting community-owned projects and sustainable development.

This essential approach was commended by Minister Costello in his address to Misean Cara's 2012 AGM: "Development intervention has to be evidence-based from the ground up rather than instigated in a top-down fashion without adequate knowledge of and consultation with the community." That perspective and the impact of missionaries' work are important in guiding Irish Aid in their reflections on the significant role of missionaries in development aid.

Missionaries' sensitivity to cultural and religious differences and commitment to the poor makes it possible to willingly remain within communities under threat from violence, natural disasters or other dangers. It is also recognised that the integrity of missionaries has earned trust, not only for the various missionary groups, but also for Ireland as a nation, hence, the ready and warm welcome with which Irish citizens and political leaders are received throughout the world. The Irish government and some business leaders also acknowledge that the role played by missionaries has helped Irish trade overseas. In international relations, reputation of a country and its people is foundational. Ireland, as a small country, has a uniquely positive reputation globally, and the Irish missionaries can be proud of their contribution to that.

The Irish government places missionaries as valued partners in Ireland's development aid programme. Missionaries give geographical spread to that programme across over 50 countries and into many remote regions where other agencies do not operate. In the reality of the diminishing numbers of Irish missionaries, therefore, it is important "to continue to support local indigenous missionaries in seeking solutions to the perennial problems of poverty and inequality," as stated by Minister of State, Joe Costello in 2013.

Most Irish missionaries are ageing, and the responsibility for ensuring continuity of their development work is being taken on by younger non-Irish religious. Congregations based in Ireland are strengthening these younger members more and more to meet the increasing demands of donors and best practices learned through experience and training in authentic development activities. This capacity building and networking has increased significantly in recent years.

While the membership is changing, the values and guiding principles for the missionary approach to development continue to inspire the non-Irish members of missionary congregations. The diversity of nationalities in missionary groups is, in itself, evidence of the positive impact of the Irish missionaries. The diverse membership is a clear sign of sustainability in that the work started by Irish missionaries will continue to bear fruit through the participation of local and indigenous missionaries in Africa, South America and Asia. That which is viable is capable of continuing its effectiveness.

While business people invest their resources in business enterprise, missionaries invest the future of ministries in their successors who will carry on their vision and values. The reality now is that women and men from above continents are increasing in numbers in most congregations. The trust placed in us non-Irish missionaries is a tribute to our own integrity, and we have an obligation to prove both competency and value for money to those who support our development work for the very poor and deprived.

As missionaries, and irrespective of our country of birth, we can easily identify with the core values, mission, goals and priorities of the 2006 White Paper and the

One World, One Future policy of Irish Aid as they resonate with our own fundamental values. Continuing to fund non-Irish missionaries in the decades ahead, therefore, is part of the Irish legacy of Meitheal (working together for the benefit of all).

The legacy of Ireland's missionaries will not die. It is being carried on in the people they trained – the new breed of missionaries and their lay associates. This is a great honour for us, the non-Irish. We bring to the missionary life the richness of our own cultures and our deep knowledge of the people we serve and live amongst. In my own case I am involved in development work in a densely populated slum area in Lusaka where I live. With the help of Misean Cara and other partners, I built a high standard secondary school which is uplifting the standards of life for the children in this deprived community.

We, therefore, affirm the need for a continued partnership with missionaries who carry on the development work initiated by Irish. We acknowledge the need to adhere to agreed standards of practice and operation which emphasise value for money, accountability, transparency and impact of aid. *One World, One Future* affirms the need to collaborate with missionaries and we hope that missionaries, Irish or non-Irish, will continue to be "an integral part of Ireland's overseas aid programme," as promised by the Minister of State, Joe Costello.

MSC students from Nicaragua, Gautemala, El Salvador and Dominican Republic studying theology in El Salvador, meet Fr. Michael O'Connell (2nd on left) of the Irish MSC Province during his visit in 2015
MSC Mission Support Centre, Cork

Sr. Loice Kashangura is a Franciscan Missionary Sister for Africa. A native of Zimbabwe, she holds a BA in Theology & Anthropology and an MA in Faith & Culture. Currently, she ministers in Zambia where she lectures in cultural anthropology and philosophy of culture at a multi-cultural Franciscan college, and in cultural studies in world religions at Kalundu Study Centre.

III

Continuing the Legacy into the Future

This book has explored how the understanding of mission has evolved and changed over the years. In the 1970s, it was *Ad Gentes* (to the peoples), now it is often described as *Inter Gentes* (between the peoples), as mutuality and universality in a global church are understood more deeply. Mission is no longer a one-way relationship. In this new era, Irish religious congregations, societies and institutes have been searching for an identity relevant for today and into the future. This year saw the merger of the IMU and the Conference of Religious in Ireland to form the Association of Missionaries and Religious in Ireland (AMRI). An objective is to animate spirits and to inject new dynamism into religious and missionary life in

Irish Aid officials visiting the FMSA Sisters in the Hands of Care & Hope Centre at Kariobangi, Nairobi in 2016. L to R: Garvan McCann, Deputy Head of Mission, Ambassador Vincent O'Neill, Sr. Miriam Duggan, Michael Gaffey, Director General, Irish Aid, and Emma Leonard, Bilateral Cooperation Unit, Irish Aid
Irish Embassy, Kenya

a different environment where new structures are needed.

The achievements of the Irish missionary movement in the Global South are simply immeasurable – from spreading the gospel message to helping and empowering the poor and vulnerable through education and skills to sustain themselves with dignity. It has worked to eliminate dependency wherever possible. It has enriched the Catholic Church in Ireland, making it a more global church. It has helped to shape Ireland's overseas aid programme. It has created an international reputation for Ireland. The experiences – harsh or otherwise – enriched the lives of missionaries themselves as servants of God.

The legacy is both extensive and diverse. As that legacy is being carried forward by a new generation of missionaries and lay associates, the movement is entering a new era as these successors shoulder a heavy responsibility with fewer resources than their predecessors. In the words of Pope Francis to the faithful during the *Year of Consecrated Life* in 2015, this new generation: "Look to the past with gratitude, live in the present with passion, and embrace the future with hope."

Speaking at the AGM of Misean Cara on 27 May 2015, President Higgins expressed his confidence in the movement when he said: "I am confident your missionary endeavour will continue to adapt to the need for new, integrated and culturally appropriate development which will support and enable the imagining and crafting of individual development pathways, for different peoples in differing contexts while preserving its core values; values which are inclusive of all humanity." His emphasis on preserving core values was very significant.

On 12 February 1999, Mary McAleese, then President of Ireland, delivered a paper on *Mission – A Hand of Friendship across the Divide* to SEDOS in Rome. Her prophetic words in a world damaged by conflict, prejudice and inequality remain as true today as they were then: "More than anyone, you have great insight, distilled from your experience, that what the world needs most of all is the loving touch of God, not empty recitations from some rulebook. More than anyone, you are well placed to bring this message to a world still locked in conflict and prejudice."

Ireland – the Catholic Church community and the state – helped over many decades to build different parts of the great legacy. It too has a responsibility to continue material support and prayerful encouragement so that a longer term positive legacy from that work can be achieved and that further connection with Ireland for the congregations in the Global South will be a reality, with mutual benefits and enrichment.

This book and exhortations elsewhere have illustrated the types of support these new missionaries will need to be sustainable and successful in their mission across the divide.

Acronyms and Glossary of Terms

AEFJN: Africa Europe Faith and Justice Network

AFJN: African Faith and Justice Network

AMRI: Association of Missionaries and Religious in Ireland

CAFOD: The Catholic Agency for Overseas Development in England and Wales

Charism: The distinct spirit that animates a religious congregation and gives it a particular character

CIDSE: Coopération Internationale pour le Développement et la Solidarité, a collection of Catholic development organisations, which can be translated as International Cooperation for Development and Solidarity

Congregation: An umbrella term used here to denote members of institutes of consecrated life and societies of apostolic life in the Catholic Church

CP: Congregation of the Passion of Jesus Christ

CVC sector: The community, voluntary and charitable sector

DAC: Development Aid Committee of the Organisation for Economic Co-Operation and Development (OECD)

Dóchas: The Irish Association of Non-Governmental Development Organisations.

ECOSOC: Economic and Social Council of the UN

EEC: The European Economic Community, now called the European Union (EU)

FBO: Faith-based organisation. The term is used here interchangeably with faith-inspired organisation, and in the context of the recognised religions of the world

Formation: The training that individuals undertake during their initiation into the life and ministry of a congregation of priests, brothers or sisters

Global South: Developing countries that are located in the southern hemisphere, i.e. Africa, South America, and Asia

IBVM: Institute of the Blessed Virgin Mary (Loreto Sisters)

IMRS: Irish Missionary Resource Service – a company set up in 2004 to distribute Irish Aid funding to support the development work of Irish missionaries in the Global South. Its name was changed to Misean Cara in 2008

IMU: Irish Missionary Union – a collaborative of missionary sending congregations that is now absorbed into the Association of Missionaries and Religious in Ireland (AMRI)

Legacy: The work of Irish missionaries that is being continued by their successors

LM: lay missionary

LMUI: The Lay Missionary Union of Ireland

LSoSF: Little Sisters of Saint Francis of Assissi

MMM: Medical Missionaries of Mary

Misean Cara: see IMRS on previous page

Mission Today & Tomorrow Conference: A two-day international conference of missionaries held in All Hallows College, Dublin on 5 & 6 June 2013

MDF: Movimento da Defensa Favelada (movement to support slum dwellers)

MSC: Drawn from the Latin *Missionarii Sacratissimi Cordis* meaning Missionaries of the Sacred Heart

NGO: Non-governmental organisation that is independent of government

Novice: A prospective member of a congregation who is reflecting on a deeper understanding of their vocation

ODA: Overseas development aid

PaRD: Partnership on Religion and Sustainable Development

OLA: Sisters of Our Lady of Apostles

Postulant: A candidate seeking admission to a congregation. Postulancy is the phase of preparation before the novitiate

PREDA: People's Recovery Empowerment and Development Assistance

Province: A geographical unit in the structure of a religious congregation

RUN: Religious at the United Nations

SCIAF: The Scottish Catholic International Aid Fund

SDGs: Sustainable development goals of the United Nations

SEDOS: Service of documentation and study of global mission

SERVE: Summer Endeavour in a Redemptorist Volunteer Experience

SMA: Drawn from the Latin *Societas Missionum ad Afros*, meaning Society of African Missions

SSHJM: Sisters of the Sacred Hearts of Jesus and Mary

SPIRASI: The Spiritan Asylum Services Initiative

SPS: The Saint Patrick's Missionary society

SVD: From the Latin *Societas Verbi Divini*, meaning Divine Word Missionaries

SVP: The St. Vincent de Paul Society

UN: The United Nations organisation

UNAIDS: The United Nations programme on HIV/AIDS

UNANIMA: The name begins with 'UN' to represent the United Nations, and the 'ANIMA' is from the Latin word for feminine 'spirit' or 'life principle'. It is a collaboration of 21 female congregations working at the UN

UNDP: United Nations Development Programme

UNESCO: the United Nations Educational, Scientific & Cultural Organisation

UNHCR: the United Nations High Commissioner for Refugees

UNICEF: United Nations International Children's Emergency Fund

USAID: The international development agency of the USA

VIVAT: The name is derived from the Latin verb *vivere* meaning 'to live' and expresses the deep wish for all that exists: 'may s/he live, may all persons live, may all creation live'

WACFO: Women and Children First Organisation

WHO: World Health Organisation

WMI: World Missions Ireland

WWGS: WorldWise Global Schools

YSI: Young Social Innovators

About the Author

After a career in business and marketing, Matt Moran managed the MSC Mission Support Centre in Cork for ten years. He served two terms on the board of Misean Cara and was chairman for four years. He is a Fellow of the Marketing Institute of Ireland, and a Fellow of the Institute of Direct & Digital Marketing in the UK.